Risk, Survival, and Power

RISK, SURVIVAL, AND POWER

Axioms Managers Live By

Robert Kirk Mueller

With a Foreword by J. M. Juran

American Management Association, Inc.

Library of Congress catalog card number:
71-103425

Standard book number: 8144-5207-8

First printing

Foreword

THIS book started its careering path of evolution almost twenty years ago, at a Saranac seminar, when a young manager from Callery Chemical Company asked me, "What are the axioms of management?" I was unable to give him a ready-made list. "No one has ever raised that question with me. I will have to think about it."

More than a decade later I was still thinking about it, having concluded that one would have to write a book to do a real job of thinking it through. Particularly intriguing was the following potential thought sequence:

- Identify the axiomatic beliefs of managers.
- Examine these beliefs, and determine which are valid and which are defective.
- Examine the implications of the defective beliefs.
- Recommend what to do.

The potentialities were superb. Even an amateur student of human behavior soon learns that men are quite logical when reasoning from their premises. What gets them into trouble is defective premises. "It's not what we don't know; some of the things we know aren't so." What could be more exciting than to clear a path through a jungle of confusion to find this treasury of managerial truth? A book it had to be, and I put the title "The

Axioms of Management" high on my list of books to be.

I also began to sound out some industrialists, notably those with some flair for philosophic moonlighting. During one relaxing evening at the AMA Grove in Hamilton, New York, I discussed the idea at length with Mr. Mueller, who was then a Vice President of Monsanto. Out of this and subsequent discussions there emerged an agreement for a joint venture between a philosophic industrialist and an industrial philosopher.

It was the industrialist who had the most time to spare. Mr. Mueller soon out-distanced me in development of the manuscript. The gap widened until I had been lapped, again and again. So I struck my colors and ceded to him my territorial rights to the subject, which rights he has now matured into the present book.

What I did not realize was that his moonlighting adventure might lead him across the border. Evidently he is one of that strange breed of industrialists for whom the intellectual frontier finally becomes more exciting than the executive suite. During the long gestation period of the manuscript, he took advantage of an early "retirement" scheme at his company and promptly became active again. However, he stopped short of a University or free-lance second career, and entered instead the halfway house of the consulting company.

The intellectual frontiersman can have a difficult time of it with the clearance procedures of the corporation. His views on the problems of society may be at odds with the party line, or may not be germane to getting out this year's production. So he is unable to publish. He is even unable to test his views in the public forum. The resulting collection of mature and unripened views accumulates, remains bottled up, and builds up pressure. Once he is at liberty, the entire mixture rushes out in a torrent.

For Mr. Mueller, the first results of his new-found freedom are precisely such a torrent, lively, provocative, surging. To provide some sense of order he has broken it up into a dozen freshets, each concerned with some concept basic to managerial life.

His treatment of these concepts rests on a solid base of long and responsible industrial practice. However, the elaboration of each concept through a remarkable assortment of curios and snippets suggests that he has been a lifelong explorer, hunter and collector in the intellectual wilds.

All this is without shame. In his book, as well as in his travels, he has entered caves, scaled crags and otherwise impishly intruded on the private domains of assorted natural and behavioral scientists. They will protest, but it will be of no avail, for Mr. Mueller's intrusions have been in the nature of commando raids rather than as an exercise in squatter's rights. He is gone before they can mobilize to throw him out.

This disdain for the proprietors extends to their subject matter, for Mr. Mueller is no respecter of the status quo. He shines a lamp into a dark corner here, shakes up a sleeping Rip Van Winkle there, and pushes over an outhouse yonder. He does leave his calling card, but he does not wait to debate the issue at length. Instead, he is off on a new invasion, leaving a trail of assertions, challenges, and quotes from an astonishingly wide spectrum of authorities.

The specialists who have spent years examining specific concepts in detail may well protest these maneuvers, and may suggest it would be more chivalrous to remain and fight it out. That would change the character of the book from a treatise on axioms to a detailed discussion on a specific axiom. Some of this detailed discussion in microcosm is obviously in order, but will have to be left to future investigators. Mr. Mueller has opted for the broad spectrum and for axioms as a species.

It makes for a well-seasoned, swift-paced book which will be gratifying to the readers and frustrating to the critics. The critics may well have a field day with the book, but it will be hard work for them.

J. M. JURAN

Preface

THIS book is not a prescriptive effort but is rather a descriptive effort to "tell it like it is" in the powerful world of top management, which is deeply concerned with risk, growth, and survival. However one broadly defines this exciting, enervating, challenging, and lonely world of the chief executive officer, he usually lives within a relatively closed system with his formal executive cabinet and his informal network of advisers helping to direct the enterprise. His exposure to management theory is usually limited, but his exposure to crises and pressures of practical management situations is great.

Ever since the monarchs of old were replaced by constitutional forms of government, the chief executive and his key executive staff—the sovereign entity in management—have had inadequate time to study clinically certain broad areas of management practice. There have been few attempts by experienced managers to distill the essence of certain beliefs out of conventional management practices. These practices tend to be less responsive to the social, intellectual, and political conflict or control situations than they are to the economic conflict or control situations which are so obvious when doing business in the real world.

The management system today works because the executives who make up the system believe, down deep, in certain axioms whether these beliefs are explicit or implicit. Top managers often don't know of or acknowledge that they believe in any such axioms. When they stop and think about it, or are forced by circumstances to search for the basic issues and axioms which underlie their position, the more perceptive ones do divulge certain axiomatic beliefs.

This book attempts to capture some of these axioms but makes no case for their being other than part of a subtle underlying framework for the American style and philosophy of management. These axioms may give a feel of how the system works as a coherent rational framework based on common sense in managerial practice with certain overtones of emerging theory. Thus these axioms are in no way prescriptive but try to identify a foundation of plausible beliefs that go into the functional relationships of the managerial way of life and as such represent current "truths" as far as the executive is concerned.

If the book is helpful, tribute is due to the many directors, executives, managers, and fellow employees who tutored me and prescribed a course of thought and action during the days when I held active and responsible corporate line and staff positions. Dr. J. M. Juran's spur and contributions during our many discussions together have been provocative and substantial. Other management friends who freely shared their experiences during a third of a century of managerial exposure in business situations are really the authors of these axiomatic beliefs. Hopefully, these axioms will prove beneficial to practicing executives searching for some tentative philosophic foundation at this early stage of development of the management profession.

ROBERT KIRK MUELLER

Contents

PART ONE: *Risk*

  I. The Anatomy of Risk 15
  II. Managerial Instinct 33
  III. Management—Art or Science? 53
  IV. The Managementality Gap 61

PART TWO: *Survival*

  V. Survival of the Fittest 89
  VI. Executive Authority 103
  VII. The Catalyst: Profit 113
  VIII. The Social Profile 123

PART THREE: *Power*

  IX. Behavioral Basics 139
  X. The Powers That Be 161
  XI. The Resonance Factor 175
  XII. A Way of Life 199

SUMMARY

  XIII. Axioms of Management 212

INDEX 219

PART ONE:
Risk

Far better it is to dare mighty things, to win glorious triumphs, even though checked by failure, than to take rank with those poor spirits who neither enjoy much nor suffer much, because they live in the gray twilight that knows neither victory or defeat.

—THEODORE ROOSEVELT

I. The Anatomy of Risk

TEDDY ROOSEVELT, who at 43 years of age became president of the United States because of an assassin's bullet, was a dashing risk taker himself. He rough-rode the trust-busting attack on Big Business at the beginning of this century. The growing demand for reform in American social life, which was being affected by the large economic combinations in the steel and oil business, was the start of a continuing increase in the regulation of business and businessmen. This regulation and control of business has complicated the risk aspects of business to a point now where the old-fashioned entrepreneurs and individual risk takers are as scarce as Pullman porters.

On the banks of the Potomac today sits the most massive establishment in the world of people and policies, set in traditional and highly structured roles that tend to reduce individual daring and risk taking to a minimum or eliminate it entirely. This is a paradox, for those who "dare mighty things" at their own risk were and are the keystones of the competitive free enterprise system that has made our society great. The opportunity to fail, in a social sense, is becoming less and less available to the individual man, whether he be in business, government, education, the military, or the clergy.

The reduced opportunity to fail in a social sense and the rising standard of living have changed our views on the nature of failure. Failure no longer means lack of food, clothing, and shelter. Lack of outstanding achievement, with commensurate reward, is the type of failure that is germane to the management world.

Fortunately, there are still those who want the rough ride of facing alone the impersonal forces of the economy, rather than plodding along with the poor spirits in established management organizations. The job of the manager is to create values by taking risks, and this needs to be recognized and consciously applied in practice to achieve success.

As Alexander H. McFarlane put it, "While profit is an absolute necessity for corporate survival, clearly the business corporation's purposes must include something more fundamental, something which qualifies it to make a profit. That something is risk." (1) *

To be prepared to recognize a true risk situation, and differentiate it from a certainty choice or a situation of true uncertainty, is the mark of an educated and competitive manager. There is no longer justification for depending on luck for a solution to such a situation. Chance and the fortuitous solution have their place, but not here. At some point, when expert knowledge runs out and viewpoints without authority are faced, a deliberation on objective risk taking is in order, and a good executive must be prepared to take a risk when this point is reached.

---

* The figures in parentheses indicate text references, which will be found in numerical order at the end of each chapter.

The concept of risk in management assumes that there is a state in which the available alternatives are known and the probability of various outcomes occurring also is known to the risk taker—that is, measurement and prediction through probability calculations are possible.

This concept of risk distinguishes it from the concepts of certainty and uncertainty. Business administration and management are replete with situations where decisions are made with certainty. Programming, optimization of profits, and other regular problems are certainty areas in which alternatives and outcomes are known and the decision boils down to one of optimum choice. More use of advanced mathematics and computer technology has brought problems in more sophisticated areas of management into the area of certainty. Some examples have been widely publicized—for example, the advanced management techniques of the Department of Defense.

When the probabilities of outcome for some of the various alternatives are unknown and not obtainable, a state of uncertainty exists. In such situations, subjective rather than objective determinations prevail. Even here, however, with ideas created by the Reverend Bayes, an English minister with a fondness for probability, the executive may be able to convert his subjective estimates into formal probabilities and proceed with solving his problems in terms of risk.

Thus the manager must be at home, not only in the determination of a business course when faced with multiple certainty choices, but also in risk taking with all its sophisticated management techniques of probability and computer usage. And, ultimately, he must be at home in the instinctive area of decision making when uncertainty prevails.

The Margin of Error

William James divided philosophers into the tender-minded and the tough-minded. He could just as well have included business managers along with philosophers. For the manager must be tender-minded to a reasonable degree in dealing with his people, yet he must be tough-minded in dealing with decisions regarding the business areas of uncertainty that he alone must make after all the staff work on probable outcomes and alternatives is made available to him. The manager must consider the aggregate aspects as well as the single or individual consequences of his decision, whether they involve human relations problems or strictly business matters. In this he addresses himself to the margin of error that is inherent in the type of business or decision situation in which he finds himself. To recognize these margins of error and deal with them intelligently is the mark of a sophisticated manager.

Sir Simon Marks, chairman of the board of Marks & Spencer, the British clothing-store chain, demonstrated this tough-mindedness in 1957 when he encountered a salesgirl puzzling over a multipage stock-requisition form in one of the 237 Marks & Spencer stores. Neither the salesgirl nor Sir Simon could figure out the purpose of the form, which had been created years before as a pilferage check sheet. This incident triggered Sir Simon's decision to bet on people's honesty, and he began eliminating some 26 million forms in a program of "operation simplification." In all, the company weeded out a yearly crop of 120 tons of paper, and within three years after the program was initiated profits had increased 50 percent as against a gross-volume rise of 11 percent, with no apparent increase in losses. An error in this decision could have been a very large one, but Sir Simon knew that the margin of error in making this decision was sufficiently small to risk the large losses that could take place if his decision were incorrect. (2)

An error concerns failure to achieve the accuracy expected. An error may not spell complete failure; but continuous inaccuracy in achievement, or departure from the expected outcome, can create an adverse trend in business activity and affect profit, growth, and ultimate survival.

Errors in conducting business activity, while troublesome for the manager, are part of the nature of business. Recognizing that there will be errors, the decision maker must make tough-minded decisions to minimize the errors or, better, to optimize them in the interests of time and resources available.

Technological Change

Errors, of course, occur in the technical and development elements of an endeavor, as well as in its business or commercial aspects. The impact of technological change on the many ways of doing things often marks a new order of magnitude of improvement. This must be identified by management, since it often represents a great opportunity or a great threat to existing institutions.

Harvard Professor of Business Administration James R. Bright (3) has pointed out many cases—Polaroid photography, xerography, the diesel locomotive, jet engines, computers, communications satellites—as major breakthroughs championed by men who had more confidence in the technological and economic potential than could have been justified by the then available facts.

According to Professor Bright, there are four classes of error that can blind us to the implications of technological developments. These are failure of assumptions —failing to allow for further technological progress; failure of imagination—the inability to translate technical advances into material consequences; failure of vision— inability to see the interaction among various technologies and among them social, political, and economic developments; and failure of nerve—along with unwillingness to act upon the implications of our own appraisals.

One would think, with all the publicity about business decision making, elimination of errors, and computer technology, that a major reduction in business errors would take place because of the facilities now available for top business-problem analysis and decision making. However, this is not the case, according to a recent study by Rodney H. Brody of the Hughes Tool Company, who looked at a wide range of companies using computers in their business. This sample of companies was impressive. They ranged in sales from $100 million to $2 billion, and altogether owned or leased 120 digital computers. The executives interviewed were presidents, vice-presidents, and other top executives. (4)

Brody found that computers have a limited impact today, not only because certain decision areas do not lend themselves to programming, but because there is a lack of understanding and appreciation in many companies of the proper use of computers. A defensive attitude persists against this invasion of managerial decision making, and there is a general hesitancy to use them.

Those of us in managerial positions must apparently awaken our organizations to the possibilities and limitations of these new management tools if we are to manage as well as we make.

Human Errors in Business

Business errors, of course, stem in part from human errors or situations beyond the control of management. Unfortunately, man's capacity for error is great, and the kinds of errors that man usually makes are not random. Managers' errors are related to the tasks they perform and how they think while they are performing them. The modern corporation and government are now so highly structured that it is difficult to make a serious error in connection with most internal business operations or affairs of state. The concepts of line and staff organization are usually well developed, with checks and balances built in to avoid human error. In the military, from which we have inherited many of our organizational principles, there is a highly developed system for avoiding such error, although this was not always so. Rigid discipline is enforced in order to fix responsibility and to correct situations when errors do occur.

The effects of individual motivation enter into man's error making as well. Often the errors that might be expected during conditions of stress are thwarted by the counteraction of the forces of motivation to do a good job under the conditions of stress.

A good example of how the individual can cope with stress and strain can be found in the experimental work done at Wright Air Development Center to determine how much skilled precision flying a man can do continuously without any sleep. After the pilot had put his aircraft through maneuver series and instrument landings for more than a day, it was found that the observers aboard, who were masterminding the experiment, were falling asleep after 24 hours. The pilot's ability to do better was a result of his motivation and dedication. (5)

Internal motivation impels leaders to perform under conditions of impairment and pressure that would cause an equivalent machine to fail completely.

For centuries man has been developing means to control the environment about himself, the mechanical and electrical creations of his inventive genius, and the intangible creations of his mind in the form of societal, military, religious, educational, and business organizations. This control has been directed at reducing error in the activities and operations of these machines and these endeavors. Very little is known about the precise nature of the human control function, despite the increasing demands for control ability in everyday life, as we operate aircraft, submarines, automobiles, trains, lawn mowers, dishwashers, chemical processes, government programs, and church, educational, and business organizations.

Although man is considered an adaptive controller, in scientific terms he can be classified as a controller who is nonlinear, error-prone, a multiple-input sampling device, and an unusually complex computer, with each man (unlike each computer) being individualistic. (6)

With man's judgment inherently error-prone, it is not surprising that when his amazing talents are used to direct a business enterprise there exists a certain margin of error, caused entirely by error-prone man himself. Add to this the possibilities of error due to the uncertain events and factors in the bubbling broth of business and we find that there is a range of error intrinsically involved in each type of business operation and that this varies considerably. It is important not so much to avoid all error as to recover and continue successfully after encountering some level of error making. If basic strategy is sound, the manager can afford errors in tactics; if overall strategy is wrong, even perfectly conceived tactics will be of no avail.

In addition to the margin of error that the manager's judgment factor may introduce, there is also a complex set of variables affecting an enterprise that make for errors of commission and omission. A cautious manager may ameliorate the effects of such business error by using financial and personnel reserves, insurance protection, and extra researching into the areas of uncertainty to reduce the extent of the unknown variables.

It is the business leader's job to decide just how far to dig into the possibilities of market research, pilot studies, trial tests, engineering design, production programming, process controls, personnel training, and other such aids to business decision making. At some point he must fish and stop cutting bait; otherwise the opportunity will escape or competitors will move in. At the moment of decision he must accept a certain margin of error, from both human and other sources, which it is uneconomical or imprudent to attempt to reduce in the time available.

Probably the best advice to follow in the subjunctive area is to avoid what Cicero described some 60 years before the birth of Christ as the Six Mistakes of Man. (7) These human errors are:

1. Believing that individual advancement is made by crushing others.

2. Worrying about things that cannot be changed or corrected.
3. Insisting that a thing is impossible because we cannot accomplish it.
4. Refusing to set aside preferences that are sheerly personal.
5. Neglecting the development and refinement of the mind; not acquiring the habit of reading and study.
6. Attempting to compel others to believe and live as we do.

Human errors in business are the same errors human beings make in other sectors of society. In business, they are exposed on the profit and loss statement or the balance sheet—if they are significant enough. Lesser errors are internally compensated for by those who did not make them, by subordinates or peers who can adjust the work or its results to obscure the errors and the effect upon profits. The errors of a person who has a habit of making them may show up only in the emotional wear and tear on him or in the effect on those who must adjust to the errors or correct them.

But a few errors *are* to be expected from leaders, even though their leadership inevitably tends to focus around the things each does best to the neglect of things he may feel less comfortable in doing and be more error-prone in doing. The Roman historian Tacitus expressed the risk that all leaders take when he said of his emperor, *"Omnium consensu capax imperii nisi imperassit."* ("Had he never been placed in authority, nobody would ever have doubted his capacity for it.")

Management Techniques

The nature of business varies so widely that different techniques are useful in the different aspects of business. In *How to Run a Bassoon Factory,* Mark Spade (a pseudonym for British humorist Nigel Balchin) differentiates "sorts of business or species of busni" as follows: "There are two main sorts of businesses. (1) Buying something and making something out of it. This is called manufacturing. (2) Buying something and making a lot out of it. This is called retailing. There is a third species known as the wholesaler or middleman, which simply buys a thing at one price, puts it in a paper bag, and sells it at another. The middleman is commonly called a Parasite, except on the Stock Exchange, where he is known as a Jobber." (8)

A serious classification of broad business activity by F. C. Mills (9) groups it into three categories:

1. The technical task of controlling energy and natural resources and handling materials. Technology is basic to this economic element of our business life. This phase of business generally submits to a quantitative approach, and statistical evaluation of the alternate means of conducting this type of activity is well established.

2. Internal organization and administration of individual business units or profit centers. In this class falls the technical function of manipulating the unit, whether it be a farm, airline, store, or factory. This function is in a relatively less organized state as far as quantitative knowledge is

concerned. Most of the key factors are subjective, qualitative, and deal with people. The behavioral scientists and sociologists are at work in this area.

3. Dealing with the uncontrollable elements that surround a business, such as the external problems of buying and selling, the economic cycle, political trends and actions, weather, acts of God, and war and peace. In this area of uncertainty there are wide margins of error in forecasting any individual factor or even the aggregate effect of the many factors that influence economics, politics, or human events.

Forecasting the Future

Management faces this sea of unforeseen economic and political activity, in its business ventures, in addition to the usual competitive forces and vagaries of consumer preference. Considerable effort has been pouring into the quest for indicators to forecast the economic-political business cycle ever since the priest-astrologer times. But the economic and political future is so complex that so far any forecasting by magic indicators is inadequate to predict the course of the economy. Hemlines of women's skirts, restaurant receipts, pari-mutuel betting volume, the level of the Great Lakes, planetary movements, and a host of both natural and man-made phenomena have been trotted out by the would-be business-cycle forecasters. Rhythmic cycles in natural phenomena; the U.S. wholesale price 54-year cycle; Schumpeter's 9-year Juglar cycles in the economic life of Germany, England, and the United States; the Federal Reserve Board's three-and-a-half-year rhythm of industrial production—these and many others have all been elements of the forecaster's armament.

Joseph, chief economist to Pharaoh, made the Bible's most famous forecast of a seven-year cycle, and similar soothsayers are still with us, using all sorts of ancient and modern indicators to foretell the course of the economy. Most of the business-cycle indicators were done in by the scholarly job of Professor Wesley C. Mitchell in a National Bureau of Economic Research study in 1961. Management either needs a qualified economist on its staff or needs to employ one in a consulting capacity to keep tuned in on economic forecasting.

The Gambling Known as Business

There is a wealth of literature available on methods other than economic forecasting for the student who wishes to explore the technique aspects of risk taking. As John McDonald says in his *Strategy in Poker, Business and War,* "A knowledge of mathematical probabilities will not make a good poker player, but a total disregard for them will make a bad one." (10)

The rapidly changing framework of decision making is making it a great deal more sophisticated than the decision making of the past half-century. We are applying techniques that completely void Ambrose Bierce's comment of 50 years ago that "the gambling known as business looks with austere disfavor on the business known as gambling." The use of statistics and probability concepts are now routine tools of the manager.

The use of mathematics in the gambling business began about 1654, when Blaise Pascal was consulted by a

businessman, Chevalier de Mere, on his gaming problems. Although LaPlace, Gauss, Poisson, and others later
turned to mathematics in scientific and social studies, it
was not until 1900 that any business statistics were kept
in the United States on a systematic basis. Today, the
businessman must recognize that the variables he faces
are less like those of roulette, where the outcome is determined strictly by chance, and more like baccarat, where
his skill is a factor.

A variety of techniques have been designed to deal
with what are considered rational organizational situations
but which, in reality, are only partly rational because
they are dealing with human managers and imponderable
external variables. The highly specified and clearly defined environment that allows techniques to be successfully used in making decisions is a rare situation indeed.
However, it is useful to recognize such optional choices
where possible.

The Lonely Decision Maker

Sigmund Freud once observed that, in all the really
fundamental issues of life, the final decision is best left to
feelings. It is the inner feeling of the manager that finally
triggers the decision to be made. The raw material of his
decision making should be information, gathered and
collated in such a way that the alternates are clearly defined, even if all the consequences are not determinable in
quantitative terms. Instinct plays an important role here,
but this inner feeling, this instinctive decision should,
whenever possible, be a conscious, deliberate action.

Practically all stages of the managerial decision-making process are or can be communal except the final one, when the lonely decision is called for. (11) Thus:

Decision-Making Process	Means by Which Accomplished
1. Information gathering	Use of all forms of communication media; many people involved
2. Information analysis	Automated data processing systems, computers, mathematical analysis, modeling by many analysts
3. Measurement selection process to quantify alternatives; development of a conceptual program	Management staff specialists who can place rational values on most variables involved
4. Substitution of actual quantities for those algebraic elements of the program equation that can be so measured or estimated	Sophisticated, experienced management team whose members can do this in their various functional areas of expertise
5. Application of a range of reasonable quantities to those subjective elements of the algebraic equations in order to allow solution of the equation under	Top management staff that can conceptualize such a "program" with help of specialists and some rational judgments

Decision-Making Process	*Means by Which* *Accomplished*
a range of extremely improbable circumstances	
6. Determination of final, definite course of action, having all program consequences in mind but relying on management instinct where imponderables or excessive degrees of uncertainty affect outcome	Step to be taken by chief executive or top accountable executive *alone* ("The buck stops here.")

If it were possible in all managerial decisions to use such an orderly approach to risk taking, the old law which has it that "if anything can go wrong it will" might be rejected in favor of a more modern business theorem: "If every objection must be overcome, nothing will get done." This is a hazard that is a real one as the management scientists take a firmer grip on the manager's mind. Unless the manager of the 1970s understands the capabilities and the limitations of the techniques and philosophies of the management scientist, he will run the risk of becoming the servant of the professional experts of this developing technology. He may become incapable of bringing rational judgment to bear on proposals before him, and his inner feeling for values and his instinctive judgment of the available courses of action will atrophy.

At some stage in the managerial decision-making process, the manager must rise above the technical considerations of the situation and overview the alternatives from his own lonely mental tower. Otherwise he will be, like the rogue Autolycus in Shakespeare's *A Winter's Tale,* "a snapper-up of inconsiderable trifles," and the results of his managerial regime will reflect progress of little value or importance.

This, then, is riskmanship for managers. It concerns recognition that the major purpose of the corporation is to create values by taking risks. The manager must therefore be able to distinguish among risk situations and handle them in the most sophisticated manner available, and to make that ultimate lonely decision when the chips are down and the dallying or programming is complete. Peter Drucker placed a proper focus on riskmanship when he wrote that "successful businesses don't talk of minimizing—they talk of maximizing opportunity." (12)

References

¹ Alexander H. McFarlane, "Lectures on the Corporation in Contemporary Society," reprinted with the permission of *Encore* magazine (1965). Taken from *The Conference Board Record* (February 1965), "The Search for Purpose," an article based on a speech delivered in 1965 as the first of a series of annual addresses at Tufts University.

² Walter A. Kleinschrod, "The Trend to Administrative Risk Taking," *Administrative Management,* Andrew Geyer McAllister, Inc. (July 1965).

³ James R. Bright, *Harvard Business School Executive Letter* (July 1967).

⁴ Rodney H. Brody, "Computers in Top-Level Decision Making," *Harvard Business Review* (July–August 1967).

⁵ John W. Senders, "Human Performance," *International Science and Technology* (July 1966), pp. 56–68.

⁶ Frederick A. Muckler and Richard W. Obermayer, "The Human Operator," *International Science and Technology* (July 1964), p. 56.

⁷ Lynde C. Steckle, *The Man in Management* (New York: Harper & Bros., 1958), p. 67.

[8] Mark Spade, *How to Run a Bassoon Factory or Business Explained and Business for Pleasure* (London: Hamish Hamilton, 1950), pp. 15–16.

[9] F. C. Mills, *Statistical Methods* (New York: Henry Holt & Co., 1924).

[10] John McDonald, *Strategy in Poker, Business and War* (New York: W. W. Norton & Co., Inc., 1950).

[11] Melvin Ashen, "Managerial Decisions," in John T. Dunlop, ed., *Automation and Technological Change* (New York: Prentice-Hall, Inc., 1962), pp. 66–83.

[12] Peter F. Drucker, *The New Society* (New York: Harper & Bros., 1949).

Additional Readings

David C. McClelland, Chapter 7, "Characteristics of Entrepreneurs," in *The Achieving Society* (Princeton: D. Van Nostrand Co., Inc., 1961).

J. D. Batten, *Tough-Minded Management* (New York: American Management Association, 1963).

Edward R. Dewey and Edwin F. Dakin, *Cycles, the Science of Prediction* (New York: Henry Holt & Co., 1947).

James G. March and Herbert A. Simon, *Organizations* (New York: John Wiley & Sons, Inc., 1958).

Technological Forecasting in Perspective (Paris: Organization for Economic Cooperation and Development, 1967).

Robert Kirk Mueller, *Effective Management Through Probability Controls* (New York: Funk & Wagnalls Co., 1950).

II. Managerial Instinct

IT was Oscar Wilde who said, "Women do have a wonderful instinct about things. They can discover everything except the obvious." However, instinct in managerial affairs is neither confined to the women of the office nor obviously characteristic of the male manager.

The administrative environment of twentieth-century business is becoming increasingly complex; the number of variables and areas of uncertainty reach even beyond the conceptual and executional ken of men assisted by computers. After all the alternates are weighed, the ingredient of managerial instinct in decision making often tips the balance in favor of success. This capability, while undoubtedly possessed by many, is exercised by few and not often recognized as the obvious plus quality of the individual.

Origin of Instincts

Webster defines *instinct* as a natural aptitude or knack and distinguishes it from *habit* in that instinct is not dependent on the individual's previous experience. Although several of the older metaphysicians compared instinct in the animal kingdom with habit, it was Darwin who pointed out that this only gives an accurate notion of the frame of mind under which an instinctive action is performed; it does not necessarily indicate its origin. Darwin also reasoned that under changed conditions in life there should be no difficulty "in natural selection, preserving, and continually accumulating variations of instinct to any extent that was profitable."

In comparing the mental powers of man and the higher animals, Darwin theorizes that their fundamental intuitions must be the same, but perhaps man has somewhat fewer instincts than those possessed by the animals which come next to him in the series. "A high degree of intelligence is certainly compatible with complex instincts. . . . There seems even to exist some relation between a low degree of intelligence and a strong tendency to the formation of fixed, though not inherited, habits. . . ." (1)

The power of reason and that of instinct are difficult to distinguish from each other. Dr. Isaac Israel Hayes, in *The Open Polar Sea*, repeatedly remarked that his dogs, "instead of continuing to draw the sledges in a compact body, diverged and separated when they came to thin ice, so that their weight might be more evenly distributed. This was often the first warning which the travelers received that the ice was becoming thin and dangerous." (2)

Psychologist A. H. Maslow links the origin of instinct to one of many motivational factors, particularly as this applies to management matters. Maslow contends that motivation theory must be "anthropocentric rather than animalcentric" and defines the concept of instinct as a motivational unit in which the drive, the motivated behavior, and the goal object or the goal effect are all appreciably determined by heredity. "As we go up the phyletic scale there is a steady trend toward disappearance of the instincts so defined." In modern man the concept of instinct is submerged in many other overlapping patterns of reaction and behavior, and it is the rare individual that can release these inborn instinctive capabilities.

Maslow goes on to point out that historically the paradigm for instinct theorists has been animal instinct. This has led to various mistakes, including the failure to look for instincts unique to the human species. "The one most misleading lesson, however, that was learned from the lower animals was the axiom that instincts were powerful, strong, unmodifiable, uncontrollable, unsuppressible. However true this may be for salmon, or frogs, or lemmings, it is not true of humans." In our complex business environment the emergence of instinct as a controlling factor becomes more involved.

More recently, Maslow has suggested a political explanation for instinct as contrasted to learning processes, since to refer to human instincts is to damn oneself as a reactionary, whereas devotion to learning labels one as liberal, progressive, and securely democratic. (3)

Primary Instincts Plus

Early social psychologists cited seven primary instincts —propensities or impulses—and related them to seven primary emotions:

1. Instinct of flight and emotion of fear.
2. Instinct of repulsion and emotion of disgust.
3. Instinct of curiosity and emotion of wonder.
4. Instinct of pugnacity and emotion of anger.

5. Instinct of self-abasement and emotion of subjection.
6. Instinct of self-assertion and emotion of elation.
7. Instinct of parental nature and emotion of tenderness.

These were later supplemented by four other primary instincts: reproduction, gregariousness, acquisition, and construction.

With tongue in cheek, Shepherd Mead says that there is another natural instinct that young women have in these more modern times. He warns the young businessman: "Temptations will be on all sides. As soon as you are eligible, girls will know it. When asked how, scientists throw up their hands. How does the salmon know to swim upstream to spawn, or the robin to build its nest? It is a deep-seated instinct, part of the wonderland of nature." (4)

In a more serious vein, Robert Ardrey's inquiry into the animal origins of property and nations, *The Territorial Imperative,* concludes that instinctual forces such as that of the salmon to return to its spawning ground, or of humans and their attachments to private territorial properties, are the source of many forms of behavior in matters of relations among individuals, organizations, and nations. This provocative concept challenges our assumptions of human uniqueness and supports instinct as a significant factor different from learning, despite our lack of knowledge of these factors in human behavior.

Ardrey considers instinct a genetically determined pattern that informs the individual how to act in a given situation. In the evolution of vertebrates, instinct has become increasingly open. "The open instinct, a combination in varying portions of genetic design and relevant experience, is the common sort in all higher animal forms." He likens instinct to the programming of a computer. In the insect world, there is a total programming in which learning plays no part; this, however, is not the case in the world of man. (5)

In the 1920s there was a complete rejection of instinct as a factor in human motivation. What was then favored was that conditioned reflex called experience. It was in the 1930s that closer attention to instinct in the world of vertebrates revived earlier considerations of genetically determined behavior, first recorded in 1898 by C. O. Whitman at a Woods Hole, Massachusetts, lecture series. The landmark paper, in 1937, was Konrad Lorenz's "The Companion in the Bird's World," which revealed that in the backboned world of the vertebrate, problems of instinct could not be reduced to the programmed specifics of insect life. Currently, there is an awakened interest in instinct as a factor in human behavior; as management science progresses along with behavioral science, a synergism may well develop from a combination of the axioms that emerge from these studies.

The reorientation that is beginning to take place in the so-called soft sciences is a result of the failure of traditional methodology in social sciences to deal effectively with the complexity encountered today. Among the more pragmatic approaches of operations analysis is the systematic utilization of the intuitive judgment of a corps of experts. Dr. Olaf Helmer of the RAND Corporation (6) describes the Delphi technique as a series of questionnaires interspersed with information and opinion feedback from previous questionnaires. The Delphi approach derives its importance from the realization that projections into the future are largely based on the personal expectations of individuals, rather than on predictions derived from established theory. Studies are now under way under the auspices of the RAND Corporation to refine and maximize the use of the intuitive input in the absence of an adequate theoretical base on which to operate in these sociological and cultural areas.

Although psychologists are in agreement that there are a relatively small number of primitive instincts that are directly or indirectly prime movers of all human activity, what we might term *managerial instinct* is a subtle capability that is discernible in the complex environment of modern-day business. This particular propensity for successful decision making is exhibited by certain managers prior to their individual experience in the managerial situation at hand. It can best be termed *instinctive managerial action*.

There is a distinction to be made between instinct and intelligence in a manager's makeup. Psychologists consider instinct a predetermined and automatic response to given external stimuli. Such an inborn response need not first be learned or acquired through training and is entirely different from the concept of intelligence quotient.

Lord Nuffield, the former leader of Morris Motors Ltd., was an impulsive and impatient executive who was ill at ease in the formal management meetings of his staff. He preferred to deal individually with people on their separate problems, and he often appeared to act both instinctively and unpredictably on major business decisions. The failure of some of these major decisions—those having to do, for example, with the Birmingham-built Empire car in 1927, the attempts to foster an export market in Australia, and some of his less successful, joint ventures with American and French firms—only serves to put the spotlight on his many fabulously successful instinctive decisions, which created and developed the Nuffield organization during the boom years in the motor industry in the United Kingdom. (7)

Decision making on the part of management leaders is a key activity—in fact, the main activity. The head of a growing business can no longer depend primarily upon "seat of the pants" decisions, but must call upon many areas of study, such as behavioral psychology, systems theory, information theory, history, economics, and mathematics, to help him compete in his decision activity. If he has managerial instinct, this will give direction to his study and point out the correct decisions.

With the complexities tending to overwhelm the mental capacity of a single mind, an improved order of guidance in decision activity is derived from group effort. A combination of these new study areas provides the primary approach to a decision, with the final thrust seasoned by instinct.

Instinct and Intuition

There is a subtle difference between instinct and intuition. The adjective *instinctive* connotes innate impulsive or spontaneous aptitude; the adjective *intuitive* implies direct perception or apprehension without apparent reasoning. Holbrook Jackson calls intuition "reason in a hurry," underlining the fact that intuition does have a reasonableness about it.

The instinctive ability of certain managers to solve their problems on an unreasoned, uninstructed, inexperienced basis is demonstrated by their tendency to cut spontaneously through complex management problems to grasp the heart of the matter. Instinct allows the manager to proceed with utter self-confidence toward resolution of the areas of uncertainty in which he has had no experience or learning. Intuitive ability is something else; although closely related to instinct, it lacks the impulsive nature of instinctive ability.

Professor Cabot of the Harvard Business School once said that a good executive is one who is able to oversimplify his problems. Although this may be more of an intuitive than an instinctive talent, the ability to pick the significant factor in a situation spontaneously, without going through the rigors of deducing it through a logical chain of reasoning, identifies a true managerial talent. Former U.S. Secretary of Commerce John T. Connor exhibited such talent when he was asked about reorganizing the Commerce Department shortly after his appointment in early 1965. He pointed out that, as a "student of management, I'm going to simplify."

The ability to jump to the crux of the matter while the rest of the crowd are still trying to define the problem is a rare gift—albeit, sometimes, a risky one. Only certain managers possess this to a degree that results in a high batting average on executive decisions.

Instinctive behavior is made up of a permanent chain of actions that are sometimes very complicated, that are always very specialized, and that seem to follow rigidly from one another. This "natural" behavior is directed toward ends of which the individual often seems ignorant or unaware at the time.

The Limitations of Instinct

Although instinct and habit are usually powerful aids to intelligent managerial behavior, in the most difficult management problems instinct is not always an infallible guide to executive decisions. Perhaps Sewell Avery's instinctive restraint on the expansion of Montgomery Ward, both before and after the financial difficulties that the company successfully weathered in a particularly tough business cycle, is illustrative of a situation where the instinct factor should not have been allowed to tip the balance of the decision-making process.

Was not Charles M. Schwab's decision to put the head office of Bethlehem Steel Corporation in the sleepy Lehigh Valley town of Bethlehem, Pennsylvania, a manifestation of instinct for a subtle but pervasive management shift needed at that period of the company's history? This was in the early part of the century, shortly after Schwab took over the helm of the company, and this move kept all the employees single-mindedly concentrating on Bethlehem's business. For a long period it was a source of management strength, but later it became an Achilles heel as the isolation resulted in a totally inside-run organization and the world competitive situation changed. Apparently, at this later time, instinct missed recognition of the timing of a new order of things and the need for external orientation of the company, its board, and management. A later chief executive, Edmund F. Martin, took action on this imbalance and made other major management changes to effect the current renaissance of Bethlehem Steel Corporation.

David Braybrooke of Dalhousie University expresses

his view of intuition in this way: "The executive does not compete with the expert in drawing conclusions from information, but forges ahead of the latter when reasoning fails and 'intuition' must be relied on; it is not the executive's business to draw conclusions at all—he is not required to meet that sort of test." (8)

Braybrooke indicates that the successful executive possesses special skill in dealing with imperfect information in an imperfect organization, and that this talent is "associated with indispensable traits of character (though none of them may be distinctive as executive types). This association is one of the things that lead people to speak of intuition in such connections. . . . To speak of intuition is just to say: A successful executive makes appropriate decisions, we know not how."

Our business world is so complex that, computers or not, instinct and intuition are still extremely valuable attributes of a good manager. However, recognition of the limitations of instinct and intuition, as well as their contributions, is important. Chester I. Barnard (9) has made some interesting estimates of the variations in intuitional factors among common vocations. He regards the major emphasis in composition of minds required as follows:

> *The Scientist:* His work requires the mastery of the technique of rigorous logical reasoning, especially in the mathematician. Nevertheless, all the able and the great scientists seem to possess nonlogical, highly intuitional mental processes.

> *The Statesman:* Balanced mental processes, but emphasis on the intuitional.

The Engineer: Initially the logical processes predominate in the strictly technical field; but in the major engineering positions, the intuitional processes may need to predominate, because commercial and economic considerations become very important, and exposition and persuasion are frequently controlling requirements.

The Junior Executive: Nonlogical processes chiefly necessary, except in the highly technical fields.

The Major Executive: Logical reasoning processes increasingly necessary, but are disadvantageous if not in subordination to highly developed intuitional processes.

Brigadier General Robert Wood Johnson (Retired), former chairman of the board of Johnson & Johnson, built many a legend around himself with some of his impulsive actions and his brand of management philosophy, which was 30 years ahead of its time. His instinct for a balance of simplicity and beauty of factory facilities and equipment, human engineering, decentralization, young staff, cost-consciousness, and housekeeping set Johnson & Johnson on a growth course that paced the industry around the world.

General Johnson employed a sculptor to streamline Johnson & Johnson's industrial equipment and effect a compromise between his dream machines and the practical limitations of machine design. In addition, he experimented with all-white concrete floors for the reason that "every speck of dirt on a white floor will challenge management's housekeeping instincts." Few of his instinctive actions, at first encounter, can be termed normal or logical.

Executives who believe that the principles of professional management do not apply to creative areas of business operations or to ultimate decision making prefer to credit their hunches or instinct or intuition when explaining the management process they employ in creative work or in the flashes of inspiration whereby they reach a major decision. A problem arises, of course, if the executive does not recognize the limitations of his instinct, intuition, or "gut-syndrome." David Ogilvy, president of Ogilvy and Mather, puts it neatly this way: "People will tell somebody that their gut-feeling was responsible for a success; you seldom hear somebody admit that his gut-feeling was responsible for failure."

Instinct in People Problems

It must be acknowledged that instinct in matters managerial is only a single factor among many in the complex relationships that exist among people involved in a business situation. Since management matters are predominantly people matters, instinct in people problems covers the widest possible application of managerial instinct.

The late Erwin Schell (10), in discussing the wide range of "mutuality relationships" that administrators have with their subordinates, reveals four potential agreements that exist in such understandings and constitute the fabric of people relations. It is in such "agreements" that the application of managerial instinct may be of value. These agreements are security in return for leadership; loyalty in return for enjoyable relations; opportunity in return for zeal; and, the most lofty of all, devotion. If the aims are high enough to inspire this emotion of the leader and the led to a plane of moral equality, this last factor of leadership requires an instinct for such principles that will incite the inner man to work cooperatively toward a specific accomplishment.

A true manager will possess an instinct for these principles, and this trait has been identified statistically in studies of key managers and their personal attributes. For example, Donald A. Laird's nationwide survey of executive traits at the Colgate Psychological Laboratory tagged a list of 500 traits considered to be most important in successful executive leadership, and from these he derived a composite hallmark of the get-things-done manager that pricked many a bubble about criteria for success in business. A "comer" disclosed, among other things, such "a marked judgment of men and judgment of events" that he is "able to anticipate future changes and developments. He has an innate and active desire to plan and organize the work of others." (11)

With this innate ability and desire, a manager can exhibit his instinctive judgment capabilities in experiences with men and events. Dr. Martin Grotjahn, in recent behavioral studies, states that this understanding of one person for another is not mysterious or uncanny. "It is not in contrast to scientific understanding. All of us once had the gift of 'listening with the third ear.' We lost it in later life, and we lost it under the impact of our education, which is aimed so much at rational thinking. We have learned how to use our logic, our reason, our intelligence, our objective observation; we have lost the ability to trust our unconscious communication with the unconscious of our friends and fellow men." (12)

The problem faced in modern management is that of identifying instinctive and intuitional capabilities in a manager and consciously encouraging their exercise at the proper time, with some measure of feedback and evaluation so that these talents can become more useful for the manager. A. H. Maslow (13) has stated the problem in this way:

> Education, civilization, rationality, religion, law, government have all been interpreted by most as being primarily instinct-restraining and suppressing forces. But if our contention is correct, that instincts have more to fear from civilization than civilization from instincts, perhaps it ought to be the other way about (if we still wish to produce better men and better societies); perhaps it should be at least one function of education, law, religion, etc. to safeguard, foster, and encourage the expression and gratification of the instinctoid needs. . . . We do have a nature, a structure, a shadowy bone structure of instinctoid tendencies and capacities, but it is a great and difficult achievement to know it ourselves. To be natural and spontaneous, to know what one is and what one really wants, is a rare and high culmination that comes only rarely and with great good fortune.

William B. Given, Jr., former president of American Brake Shoe Company, was an impatient, quick-acting boss, whose success story pivots around his instinctive ability to train men with unique techniques of his own. He had a knack of decentralizing his management to a point that developed managers to their highest potential. His instinctive methods have been characterized as those of a prize-fighter trainer: "He sparred with his subordinates, danced rings around them, and so taught them to handle themselves and develop their capacities to the full. His ideas of teaching were never to tell, but to teach men how to think." A typical impulsive technique of Given was to ask in whoever was waiting in his office anteroom when one of the managers was expecting to see him in private on a project. This was a calculated maneuver; it was one thing to sell an idea to Given and another to sell it with an audience present. Often the invitee demolished the idea and spared Given that job without embarrassment in handling his subordinate.

Given's instinct for tapping the power of bottom-up management, without relaxing top management responsibility for overall results, was a stirring experience for the younger executives in American Brake Shoe Company, who appreciated his instinctive feeling for sparking their potential, his tolerance toward failure, and his emphasis on accomplishment.

Alex Bavelas (14) makes a useful distinction between the idea of leadership as a personal quality and the idea of leadership as an organizational function that recognizes this factor of managerial intuition or instinct:

> Early notions about leadership dealt with it almost entirely in terms of personal abilities. Leadership was explicitly associated with special powers. An outstanding leader was credited not only with extensions of the normal abilities possessed by most men, but with extraordinary powers such as the ability to read men's minds, to tell the future, to compel obedience hypnotically. These powers were often thought of as gifts from a god, as conditional loans from a devil, or as the result of some accidental supernatural circumstance attending conception, birth, or early childhood. Today, claims of supernatural powers are made more rarely, but they are not entirely unknown. Of course, milder claims—tirelessness, infallibility or intuition, lightning-quick powers

of decision—are made in one form or another by many outstandingly successful men. And when they do not make them for themselves, such claims are made for them by others, who, for their own reasons, prefer such explanations of success to other more homely ones.

Outright supernatural explanations of leadership have, in recent time, given way to more rational explanations. Leadership is still thought of in terms of personal abilities, but now the assumption is made that the abilities in question are the same as those possessed by all normal persons; individuals who become leaders are merely presumed to have them to a greater degree.

All successful managers have as an attribute some measure of managerial instinct, which comes into play at the critical time after logical and rational analysis has had its inning. The batting average of the successful manager in selecting the proper alternative course of action is dependent on the exercise of managerial instinct and intuition in that lonely moment when a manager must take full responsibility for the direction in which he leads his associates.

Instinct as an Axiom in Management

All our progress is an unfolding like the vegetable bud. You have first an instinct, then an opinion, then a knowledge, as the plant has root, bud and fruit. Trust the instinct to the end, though you can render no reason.
—RALPH WALDO EMERSON

Management philosophy traditionally embraces the concept that leadership qualities and management ability are attributes that occur in differentiated form in various persons. This is postulated to such an extent that some terms—"born leader," "natural leadership," "take-charge characteristic," "promising executive"—are commonly found in appraisal records or interview reports. In addition, there is recognition that some persons possess "natural" sensitivity or intuition and certain instinctive reactions that are effective in management situations. In areas of uncertainty frequently encountered by managers, these rare talents are often the key factors in management success, albeit they are at one end of a spectrum of multiple factors that pertain to overall managerial distinction.

A good manager instinctively assumes certain axioms in a situation that has so many variables, degrees of freedom, subjective factors, and emotional aspects that it is outside the scope of normal, rational analysis. These relatively undefined bench marks of management are instinctively possessed by those managers fortunate enough to be endowed with capability in such matters. These instinctive axioms form the end point toward which the analysis of managerial problems can be directed.

The ability to use instinctive know-how in management matters is a rare quality that is recognizable in very few managers who have emerged during the management explosion of this century. If we assume that this characteristic has a biological origin, then the possibility of an optimum occurrence of genes providing these instinctive reactions is obviously a rare numerical possibility. Various estimates of the number of genes or polygenes in man run from 10,000 to 100,000. An optimum combination for reproducing "instinctive know-how" under the influence of widely varying environments would be a rare occurrence and would produce a rare manager.

Chester I. Barnard's perspective on the subjective factors is helpful here in that it considers the executive functions as parts of a process of organization. "The essential aspect of the process is the sensing of the organization as a whole and the total situation relevant to it. It transcends the capacity of merely intellectual methods, and the techniques of discriminating the factors of the situation. The terms pertinent to it are feeling, judgment, sense, proportion, balance, appropriateness. It is a matter of art rather than science, and is aesthetic rather than logical." (15)

In management affairs, the instinctive reactions of a good manager normally stimulate intelligent, timely managerial behavior. To use the language of Gestalt psychology, this behavior is "to structurally reorganize the perceptual field involved." It includes, not only those elements obvious from personal look-see or familiarity with the actual environment, but also the abstract elements of the situation that can be reasoned from intelligent possession of know-how in behavioral aspects of human relations, personality characteristics, organizational structures, business philosophy, and objectives of the enterprise.

Perhaps future advances in personnel administration will take serious note of the power and place of managerial instinct and intuition. The organizational culture in which we exist is now instinct-phobic in character. Recognizing instinct as such, and honing its edge for coping with increasing areas of uncertainty, will be a very sophisticated step in the development of individual managers who have the inborn ability to utilize instinct in the decision-making arena.

References

[1] Charles Darwin, *Origin of Species* and *Descent of Man* (available in Modern Library), Chapter VII, Chapter III.

[2] Isaac Israel Hayes, *The Open Polar Sea* (1867).

[3] A. H. Maslow, "Criteria for Judging Needs to Be Instinctoid," in A. M. Jones, ed., *International Motivation Symposium* (University of Nebraska Press, 1964).

[4] Shepherd Mead, *How to Succeed with Women without Really Trying* (London: Clark Boardman Company, Ltd., 1958), p. 35.

[5] Robert Ardrey, *The Territorial Imperative: A Personal Inquiry into the Animal Origins of Property and Nations* (New York: Atheneum Publishers, 1966).

[6] Olaf Helmer et al., *Social Technology* (New York: Basic Books Inc., 1966).

[7] Sir Miles Thomas, *Out on a Wing* (London: Michael Joseph, Ltd., 1964), Chapter 10.

[8] David Braybrooke, "The Mystery of Executive Success Re-examined," *Administrative Science Quarterly* (March 1964), pp. 553–560.

[9] Chester I. Barnard, "Mind in Everyday Affairs," *Cyrus Fogy Brackett Lectures* (Princeton: Princeton University, 1963).

[10] Erwin Schell, *Technique of Administration: Administrative Proficiency in Business* (New York: McGraw-Hill Book Co., 1951).

[11] Donald A. Laird, *How to Use Psychology in Business* (New York: McGraw-Hill Book Co., 1936), p. 163.

[12] Martin Grotjahn, *Beyond Laughter* (New York: McGraw-Hill Book Co., 1957), p. 144.

[13] A. H. Maslow, *Motivation and Personality* (New York: Harper & Bros., 1959), pp. 145, 345.

[14] Alex Bavelas, "Leadership: Man and Function," *Administrative Science Quarterly* (March 1960), pp. 491–492.

[15] Chester I. Barnard, *The Functions of the Executive* (Cambridge: Harvard University Press, 1938), p. 235.

Additional Readings

Gaston Viaud, *Intelligence, Its Evolution and Forms* (New York: Harper & Bros., 1960).
Luis J. A. Villalon, *Management Men and Their Methods* (New York: Funk & Wagnalls Co., 1949).

Science is a manner of thinking: Art is experience.

—L. A. JORDAN

III. Management— Art or Science?

MANAGEMENT is both an art and a science when it is successful. Just as a public speaker plays on the intelligence, emotions, and humor of his audience, the successful manager tries to use artful skills with a scientific management discipline. There is a refinement that can only be described as the touch of an artist that makes or breaks a manager with his peers, his colleagues, and his subordinates.

The man selected to be a manager is chosen because he does not need a manager. He does not need one because he has the intuition and training to balance art and science in his managerial conduct.

Isaac Newton once said, "O physics! Preserve me from metaphysics!"—and thus expressed the yearning that the scientifically inclined person has for all answers to be definable and clean-cut, as in the early axioms of mathematics and physics. As more knowledge was gained, however, new challenges arose to the regularly ordered world of the mathematician that was set forth in Euclid's 15 original postulates in his system of logic for the teaching of geometry. So it is, also, with the new theoretical physics, which makes the old textbook division of physics into "heat, light, sound, electricity, and magnetism," a very inadequate characterization indeed. Concepts of fundamental particles and properties of matter are rapidly changing with the leptons, mesons, baryons, and lasers, to name just a few concerns of this rapidly expanding discipline. And so it is with most scientific disciplines. Although they appear rigid, they have an ever changing balance between the discipline of physics and the more inchoate metaphysics.

With a constantly evolving scientific basis for activity, it is hardly realistic to impose on the delicate job of managing people any such rigid approach as is characterized by the popular idea of a scientific effort, as distinct from the fluid and seemingly relaxed approach of the artist or the metaphysician. The surgeon, the patrol leader, the foreman, or the president must combine with the necessary scientific discipline a measure of art that allows the management effort to be acceptable to those who must react to and interact with it. This combination is the work of a professional, who can do for his livelihood what others do for pleasure.

The managerial cult, about which so much has been written in recent years, has both an interface with the artistic and an interface with the scientific. The manager's interface with the social sciences should be fed through the scientific management disciplines, now including such classifications as mathematical modeling, measurement of the decision-making process, organizational theory and design, experimental gaming, information control, and the systems approach to organization and enterprise management. A modern manager has a double-barreled task in rising to meet these two separate interfaces.

Social Versus Natural Science

A considerable amount of foundation money is financing research in the social sciences, but great controversy still exists as to whether human nature can be scientifically studied as well as nature itself. Although human behavior may be more difficult to study, the scientific method is undoubtedly applicable to both man and his physical world.

In the early seventeenth century, a group of famous scholars used to gather at Oxford for weekly discussions in what was called the "Invisible College," which attacked the dry scholasticism of Cambridge and Oxford. Distinguished members of the Invisible College were Robert Boyle, Christopher Wren, the astronomer Seth Ward, Isaac Newton, the physicist Robert Hooke, and the King of England. As a consequence of the king's membership, the college was rechristened the Royal Society, which to the present day has stood for experiment and firsthand observation as against pure exercises in logic and unconfirmed speculations. Although the Royal Society has mainly been concerned with the physical sciences, it has initiated inquiries into social statistics as well, and it has set in motion studies of the behavior of man, population theory, actuarial science, and principles of insurance.

The natural sciences have forged ahead and reached a "stunning climax" in the atomic bomb. This feat has in turn encouraged a similar drive for accomplishment in the social sciences. The recognition of human nature as a determining factor in management practice and a vital element in management theory goes back to the turn of the century with the original work turned out by H. L.

Gantt, Lillian M. Gilbreth, R. F. Hoxie, and Mary Parker Follett, to name just a few of the pioneers. (1)

There is no doubt that science can aid and is aiding in the search for sophistication in dealing with order and disorder in human affairs as they are encountered by the manager. Writing in *Science* magazine, Van Rensselaer Potter pointed out that "mankind has an inborn desire to have some degree of organization in life, and this leads many to gravitate in the direction of religion or science, both of which are identified as mechanisms for bringing order out of disorder." (2) Despite this desire, however, a completely ordered society or management setup is not destined to succeed; there is need for some disorder to insure some balance of human nature and some variety in human affairs. Plato describes it best in his *Republic:* "democracy, which is a charming form of government, full of variety and disorder."

Valid concepts of order in terms of custom, tradition, law, morality, and the function of perturbation—a degree of disorder to evoke new, improved conditions for the conduct of human affairs—need to be studied by social scholars and management scientists to get the best of both disciplines.

Not surprisingly, the more social and natural scientists develop a dialogue, the less defined is the separation between these conceptual approaches to the conduct of human affairs in a physical world. Perhaps the most rapidly advancing front is that of information and computer technology with its physical and seemingly metaphysical manipulations, which are so useful in predicting or generalizing affairs and conduct. One of the major limitations proves to be the human interface with these new machines. New disciplines are required to get man to conform sufficiently to communicate with the machine and play through mentally, say, a simulation of a complex business or behavioral problem in order to test out alternate possibilities.

The capacity of the computer provides the opportunity for the manager to avoid being problem-oriented or machine-oriented and to become solution-oriented. Through the techniques available, the various possibilities can be examined painstakingly until a realistic solution can be defined. Someone has said that this is like "torturing an economist at the stake until he comes up with one number" to define his position.

But all this sophisticated, high-level language is recent in the management scheme of things. The common business-oriented language trails the scientific formula-translation language and is itself trailed by the newer behavioral scientists' language. Until the social scientist, the manager, and the natural scientist can communicate better, a conflict will remain.

Management's Choice

Top executives are usually touchy about their style of managing. After all, did they not acquire their status by using the style and conduct with which they feel most comfortable? A serious problem now exists because so many of the current managers at the apex of the internal power structure do not have a comfortable understanding of the world of the "soft" sciences, so recently developed. Moreover, it is difficult for them to keep up with the more classical "hard" science that prevailed and predominated during their early career growth. This is a matter of evolutionary timing, and it will remain a problem until the newer, more academically equipped managers can be exposed to the fire of management experience and take over the top positions of management power in our enterprises.

The leadership characteristics of today's top executives provide the stability of the older order of management, but they often tend to stifle the management reproduction process, with its upgrading of capable younger managers in a newer, more complex environment. A palace revolution, with the newly trained management cadre taking over entirely, would be risky, and the pendulum could swing too far. Perhaps the way out is to follow the leader, as distinct from the executive, and let the few leaders who can bridge the management gap at this time thread segments of our management fraternity through the interfaces of the new management movement.

A leader, as opposed to what the sociologists call an executive, influences a corporation more than it influences him. He tends to be a revolutionist, not an evolutionist. The executive's role is normally determined by the corporation's organization and style; the role of his own personality is limited.

We need more leaders and fewer executives in order to master management, in today's company environment of great pressures, toward coexistence with the new tools of the scientists, the sociologists, and the anthropologists. The leader who can balance this new knowledge without becoming a "yellow pages" manager—that is, one who seeks expert guidance from many sources without contributing his own input, particularly his own artistic leadership touch—can lead the way to a new plateau of management understanding. Without this touch of artistic leadership, an enterprising corporation will be gradually transformed into an arid bureaucracy.

References

[1] Ernest Dale, "The Functional Approach to Management," in *Proceedings of the Annual Meeting of the Academy of Management* (Ithaca: Cornell University, 1952).

[2] Van Rensselaer Potter, "Society and Science," *Science* (November 20, 1964), pp. 1018–1022.

Additional Readings

Olaf Helmer and Nicholas Rescher, "On the Epistemology of the Inexact Sciences," *Management Science* (1960). Also, *Social Technology* (New York, Basic Books Inc., 1966).

Claude S. George, Jr., *The History of Management Thought* (Englewood Cliffs, N.J.: Prentice-Hall, Inc., 1968).

Stafford Beer, *Management Science: The Business Use of Operations Research* (New York: Doubleday & Company, Inc., 1968).

J. M. Juran, *Managerial Breakthrough* (New York: McGraw-Hill Book Co., 1964).

Ernest Dale, *Organization* (New York: American Management Association, 1967).

Glenn A. Bassett, *Management Styles in Transition* (New York: American Management Association, 1966).

IV. The Managementality Gap

ANALYZING a situation before making vital decisions has been a practice of realistic politicians since Machiavelli made his attempts at scientific inquiry for the politically ambitious Giuliano de' Medici.

Business managers, on the other hand, constantly make decisions with inadequate information and under the pressures of insufficient time. Some make intuitive decisions, and the process stops there. The more thoughtful ones follow up, analyze the results of their decisions, and store the lessons learned in their personal memory banks for future applications. Too few managers, however, have reached the point where they follow the lead of the politicians by rigorously analyzing alternative consequences *before* choosing one solution over another.

There is a quarter-century age gap between today's top executives and the current crop of management-oriented technical graduates. Although neither party lacks sophistication, acumen, or flair, a gap does exist between the mentality of *successful managers*—who may be technically unschooled, preoccupied with competitive complexities, and justifiably nervous about management science—and the *technical turks* of the business world, those practitioners of management science who offer only limited experience in reducing theory to practice plus a certain greenness in business and organizational matters.

This gap is propped further apart by the absence of a common standardized lexicon for management practices and for management science.

The impressive powers of these two groups must get into mental lockstep. Before this can happen, however, there must be mutual understanding of the real "state of the art" of management theory and practice, the potential of management science, the behavioral framework of organization, and the forces at work in the social-business system. The demanding problems of the future will be solved only if we are able to meld the disparate talents of the charismatic intuitive leader and the management scientist.

The Management Scientist's Viewpoint

The management-oriented technical man can offer some thoughtful propositions on why, when, and where top management can multiply executive power by realistically allocating effort in the managing process. However, it is not universally agreed that there is such a subject as management science. No one yet has managed to codify the art and experience mankind has acquired in managing things. The science of the subject concerns the very nature of management itself, not the virtuosity with which a manager can perform certain techniques of management.

What is management science? A simple definition for our purpose is the application of scientific, systematic, or technical approaches to business problems; someone has called it "quantified common sense." A principal aim of management science is to increase the number of alternatives open to management, thereby increasing the likelihood of selecting the best course of action in a given set of circumstances. A basic concept of management science is that business is founded not only on unpredictability but on a deep-seated uncertainty that cannot be resolved even in theory. This concept replaces the archaic notion of the deterministic science of management which flourished in the early days of industrial engineering.

The object of management science, then, is to invent a "calculus of decision" by determining probabilities rather than certainties. Having set some parameters on possible solutions by defining his aims and objectives, the manager using management science can quantitatively examine alternate courses in advance and preview the probable results of his decision.

Both the scientist and the businessman see their world not so much as a collection of definite things as a flux of uncertain interactions. The executive does not need to know how to quantify the choices himself any more than he has to be a watchmaker in order to tell time.

In the eyes of the management scientist, there are at least six reasons why an executive should consider the use of management science:

1. To minimize the effects of surprise happenings.
2. To cope with increased complexity.
3. To minimize the impact of bad decisions.
4. To capitalize on the value of a systems approach.

5. To keep up with rapid changes.
6. To avoid the limitations of intuitive reasoning.

Surrounded by overwhelming problems, a good many managers confine their thinking and planning to conventional procedures, then are surprised when the house suddenly comes tumbling down. A sensitivity analysis, including probabilities of all possible happenings, will allow the manager to prepare alternative strategies for most probable events before they occur. Then he can devote his time to tactics; that is, determine how to behave when the event is faced—when opportunities and problems arise.

Standard Oil of California is a good example here. It has a linear programming model of production facilities and raw materials available on the shelf, with solutions to deal with disasters such as war in the Middle East, extensive fire damage, or strikes. Phillips Petroleum, for its part, has utilized hybrid computations to train supervision under simulated operating conditions to avoid surprises in the start-up of a petroleum plant.

Increased Complexity

Lincoln's executive branch at the start of the Civil War just topped 36,000 civilians compared to President Johnson's 2.8 million when the United States sent troops into Vietnam. In Lincoln's day, the United States was represented at one international conference a year, but in 1968 there were nearly 700 such conferences to cover. In the last half of the 1940s the federal government filed 529 antitrust cases compared to the 3,598 cases filed in the first half of the 1960s.

In 1939 the Code and Regulations of the Federal Income Tax had 425 pages. Today there are 3,947 pages. Monsanto's federal return ten years ago was only 66 pages long. In 1967 it was larger than the Montgomery Ward catalog—1,067 pages.

The increasing complexity of business thus is an obvious reason for executives to consider the use of management science.

The Impact of Bad Decisions

Bigness increases the significance of both good and bad decisions. The assets of the 100 largest-asset companies in 1917 were $15 billion; the top 100 in 1967 totaled $200 billion. Making mega-decisions by the seat-of-the-pants method is not good enough. Management science approaches—linear programming and simulation, for example—can afford better planning and control of variables or at least evaluate their sensitivity.

Decisions in big business require predecision evaluations as well as the experienced judgment and intuition of the top manager.

The Systems Approach

The Earl of Shaftesbury once said that the most ingenious way of becoming foolish is by a system. This is true if the user of the system is a man who builds a castle and then lives in a shack close by. The systems concept is a state of mind, an anti-piecemeal, integrative philosophy with which one must live, rather than something to be considered as a separate body of knowledge.

Starting as a problem-solving technique in the military,

the holistic systems concept was first adapted by think-tanks like Arthur D. Little, Inc. and the RAND Corporation. From there it moved to universities and into government and business. The principles are not new; they have been appreciated ever since the king's men first failed to put Humpty Dumpty together again. Anyone can design a complicated system; it takes a true manager to conceive a simple one.

Opportunities for a systems approach abound everywhere. An example: Motor trucks average some six miles an hour in New York traffic today, as against eleven for horse-drawn trucks in 1910, and the cost to the economy of traffic jams (according to a *New York Times* business survey) is $5 billion yearly! Authorities are currently struggling with an approach to this traffic-congestion problem. A systems approach would not merely design a freeway system but would also consider the implications of this traffic-congestion problem to the overall city problems of pollution, dislocation of population, schools, growth, and air transport.

A systems approach, in short, is a state of mind that is helpful in complex situations and in considering surprise-free projections.

The Rapidity of Change

That internationally known manager General De Gaulle once said, "The world is undergoing a transformation to which no change that has yet occurred can be compared, either in scope or rapidity." We can get an idea of the truth of that statement by going back to B.C.—before computers—to see how rapidly changes are occurring.

Since the development of the early electronic computer in 1946, speeds and memory capacity have increased 1,000 times, while costs per calculation have dropped about 200 times.

Computer power has come to be the new international yardstick by which the present and future potential of an industrial nation is measured. Three-fourths of the world's computers are in the United States; no other country has more than 7 percent of the total. In spite of this seeming saturation, experts estimate that we have applied only 10 to 20 percent of the potential of even our existing computer technology.

The number of patents granted can also be used as a dramatic measure of change. In the United States, 50 percent *more* patents were issued in 1966 than in 1956 in spite of turn-of-the-century fears that everything worthwhile had already been invented. In 1966, more than 410,000 patents were issued in 73 countries of the world. In the United States alone, over 68,000 patents were issued.

Our Department of Commerce states that before World War I there was a gap of 33 years between invention and application. By World War II the gap was ten years and narrowing. The laser, first conceived in 1958, was in use seven years later as a manufacturing tool and surgical instrument.

With such rapid changes taking place, one executive confides that two things worry him these days: one, that things may never get back to normal; the other, that they are already there! However, the time we live in should not be marked "subject to change without notice." For the essence of change is that it *is* noticed, and managers must be sure they are the ones who notice it first.

The Limitations of Intuitive Reasoning

It was Alfred P. Sloan, formerly of General Motors, who said that "the final act of business judgment is, of course, intuitive." Intuitive judgment is especially valuable in a situation of uncertainty which requires action but whose risks resist analysis by a calculus of probabilities. The true leadership function is one which consists of converting uncertainty into calculated risk and leading the enterprise in the "best chance" direction toward the goal.

Nothing has yet been invented to match the human brain's intuitive capacity. John von Neumann calculated that the brain can store all the inputs of a 60-year lifetime, some 2.8×10^{20} bits of information, considerably more than the current generation of computing devices. Although the brain operates a million times more slowly than present computers, it functions in a multipath fashion. Thus several trains of thought proceed at once and interact to produce alternative "intuitive" judgments.

Recently, management scientists have attempted with the Delphi technique to use the intuitive judgment of corps of experts systematically to deal with complex social science problems. We can hope that there will be applications in business areas in the future. The limitations of intuitive reasoning may become a serious problem, however, when a successful, intuitive manager relies entirely on this impulsive means to run a business.

Perhaps future advances in personnel administration will take serious note of both the power and the limitations of managerial intuition. The answer should be a proper balance of quantified-probability decision choices, seasoned with the right sprinkling of intuition and acted upon at the proper time. As Professor Max Lerner of Brandeis University puts it, "You should act as a man of thought and think as a man of action."

Having given a variety of reasons why the management scientist thinks executives should consider management science as an aid, we now should ask—

When Should Management Science Be Used?

There's a story about a ten-year-old at a progressive school in Washington who returned home with his report card. His mother asked him about his marks. "I got 28 in geography, 32 in arithmetic, and 35 in spelling, but"— and a proud smile swept over his face—"I got 95 in long-range planning!" I imagine his mother taught him what every good manager should know: It's not enough to plan for the future; we have to make a passing grade in solving our present problems.

The two most obvious cases in which the manager can apply management science techniques are (1) when he wants to control his *present* business and (2) when he wants to plan for the *future*. Available control systems for current activities are time-consuming and expensive. Simulation for future planning, however, can proceed with little data and—relatively speaking—little in the way of resources. Let's look briefly at both planning and control to see whether a proper interrelationship can be built between them in the future.

1. Management control. Operational control systems use historical data representing transactions such as customer orders placed, shipments made, and the like. The programming involved requires that data streams be captured and edited, errors recognized and corrected, totals balanced, and summary information fed to financial reporting systems. Because of their historical nature, the data are fixed. Thus it should be possible to vary the *logic* by which the system views and compares the data.

However, it has proved difficult, expensive, and time-consuming to build such operational control systems, since they depend for accuracy on an all-encompassing capture of the transaction-data streams of a company. Programming even data-*correction* routines is a major task.

Scientific management techniques such as statistical control, input-output charts, PERT, and decision trees help extend the manager's command over a complex, dispersed organization, but it is wise to determine whether you really need—or can afford—a full-blown operational control system. A more realistic approach might be to select the most urgent problem area and tackle it, with the objective of working toward an encompassing plan later.

2. Planning for the future. There are at least three kinds of planning: broad strategic planning, tactical planning, and operating or budget planning. Strategic planning is the province of the managing executive in that it entails determining objectives and combinations of alternatives for achieving these objectives. Tactical planning deals with the efficient use of resources that can be allocated to achieving an objective. Operating planning is concerned with developing a control mechanism.

In planning, as contrasted to control, the logic is fixed but the data can be varied. Igor Ansoff of Carnegie-Mellon University (1) has analyzed this process a little differently in terms of extrapolative planning and entrepreneurial planning. Management science can contribute to different degrees in these elements of the planning process however you characterize it. One advantage here is that it forces managers to follow a track in developing their plans. The strategic and tactical planning areas are the ones where managers can use systems analysis, simulation, and modeling techniques based on assumptions about the future. They do not need to build elaborate systems for data capture. It is frequently possible to design and implement a complex planning system in a relatively short time.

For example, project simulation will permit "paper tryouts" without significant dollar risks and yield fast responses to "what if" questions. In this technique, a manager makes the best assumptions he can concerning simulated events and their consequences. He can do this with limited data and his best-guess range on interacting variables and trade-offs (such as changing the time frame) and money manipulations.

Before Monsanto made a recent decision to build a 150-million-pound acrylonitrile plant at Teeside, England, the project economics were simulated in a model having about 120 variables, including location, taxes, labor costs, tariffs, and transport. More than 100 simulations were run before the business decision was made. In addition, the simulations were used beneficially in communicating with all staff functions on such matters as the effect of possible devaluations; they permitted a dynamic appraisal, over the expected life of the plant, as to its economics for the entire period.

A New York consulting firm in the field of process engineering offers a linear program for an ethylene plant at a price of $14,000. It will predict performance on any feedstock for which furnace-yield information is available, and it has more than 22 product options.

When and Where the Management Science Approach Should Not Be Applied

Enthusiasts for management sciences sometimes imply that *all* factors of the management process are fair game. This zealous misconception, perhaps the greatest cause of misunderstanding between management and practitioner, needs clarification. For example, the manager must always decide, or manage, in the selection of objectives and goals and the formation of basic policy. Personnel handling and interpersonal relationships, like eyeball-to-eyeball negotiation, also are not fit subjects for simulation or modeling.

The Top Management Viewpoint

So much for the management scientist's viewpoint as to why, where, and where not executives should take advantage of this new body of knowledge. Let's look at the situation through the eyes of the executive and see why he does not readily embrace the management sciences.

Someone once said that a manager is the man selected to be the boss because he doesn't need one. Why is it that men who meet this criterion seem to have some inherent resistance to the "new management skill"? There are a number of factors that contribute to this resistance.

1. Technical obsolescence. About 1900, the mathematical sophistication of the United States dropped drastically for causes unknown. In midcentury, Sputnik, the introduction of the new math, and the beginning of the cybernetic revolution reversed our mathematical posture. The current crop of managers, however, was spawned during the half-century of mathematical doldrums; most were only slightly influenced by mathematics during the years of their formal education. As a result, many American managers are not comfortable with mathematical approaches, nor are they what we might call symbol-oriented. While mathematics is not the only discipline in which it is difficult to keep current these days, it is representative of the advancing technical front.

More recent graduates, especially the management science breed, came out of an educational system where mathematics has been emphasized. As lately as 1963, there were only six schools in the United States with "good" management science programs. By 1968, there were good, complete programs available in 15 schools. During 1955–1965, the number of bachelor's degrees in engineering and physical science doubled, while bachelor's degrees in mathematics increased fivefold. The comparative difference in symbol sophistication between today's management-oriented, technical-college graduate and the middle-aged senior executive is a major cause for the current lack of understanding between the two groups.

At the rate of change under way, a manager has a "half-life" of about ten years: Half of what he knows will be obsolete in the next decade, or—to say it another way—half of what he will need to know in ten years is not now available to him.

Only a limited amount of adult education in management science theory has been possible. One reason for this is the fact that the discipline is so recent, even in educational institutions. As a specific example, 80 percent of Dartmouth's undergraduates now get personal experience in computer language and operation.

A profile of industrial chief executive officers shows that in 1967 only 6 percent of presidents had engineering and scientific specialist backgrounds. Five years earlier, the proportion had been 16 percent. The primary route to the top (for 29 percent of presidents) was through general administration.

The profile did indicate that *engineering* was the most popular undergraduate major subject for all executives, while business subjects rated second. However, the average age of these men—55—indicates that they graduated in the depths of the Depression or in the threshold years of World War II, well before the management science approach to business problems was a reality.

2. Communications problems. Fortune editors once proposed that "if business has a new motto, 'communicate or founder' would seem to be it." Communications may cement an organization or disrupt it, and the first function of an executive must be to develop and maintain an effective communication system.

Unfortunately, the average executive does not understand the language of the management scientists. This is nothing new; Goethe called mathematicians "a sort of Frenchmen," and he went on to say "when you talk to them, they immediately translate it into their own language and right away it is something utterly different."

Much earlier, when science was in the hands of alchemists, symbols served as much to conceal information from outsiders as to convey it to those who could read them.

There is, one fears, a little of the alchemist in the management scientist. When the chief executive does not believe the sales manager's forecast, the management scientist may try to help by suggesting the use of, say, Wald's minimix criterion, Savage's regret criterion, Hurwicz's coefficient of optimism, or the Laplace-Bayes criterion based on the principle of insufficient reason. Can you blame the dismayed senior executive for refusing to apply such esoteric terms to his nonforecastable system? Deciding to draw his own conclusions, he will probably say: "Let's get on with it. I'll gamble on Joe's sales forecast if he cuts it in half, because I've a hunch he'll sell that much. And, besides, I don't know what you young fellows are talking about!"

So, if you can offer some helpful technique in a situation like this, don't hide a pint of seed in a peck of chaff! Anthony Hope Hawkins, the English novelist, once said, "Unless one is a genius, it is best to aim at being intelligible." Were Hawkins living today, he would surely urge all young technical people to communicate in terms the executive receiver can comprehend.

3. *Computer mystique.* The danger of the computer is not the science-fiction fear that machines will begin to think like men, but the more realistic apprehension that men will begin to think like machines. Artificial intelligence is inhuman. It does not grow or have an emotional base, and it is shallowly motivated. And, whereas these defects may not be important in technical decisions, they are very important when social decisions must be made.

There is also a myth founded on the implicit assumption that, after a few technical problems are solved in management information systems, the top and middle executives will have a vastly simplified job—if their job exists at all. The sleeper in this picture, of course, is the fact that successful managers got where they are on criteria that the computer cannot satisfy. They have demonstrated an ability to make sound decisions from among several "what if" choices, to deal creatively with novel situations, and to get things done through other people—in a word, to manage.

To set at least some managers' minds at rest, the name of the game is really not "computer" but "modeling." Without knowing it, managers have been doing subconscious modeling in their heads for years in an informal nonrigorous way. This has served, at least in part, to optimize their decisions. Today's business, however, is often too intricate and complex to rely on implicit mental modeling alone, and here is where a computer can help.

There is, moreover, another incidental but often large benefit to computer modeling. When the manager builds the model, he is forced to be painfully explicit and exact, and he often uncovers areas of ignorance. This demand for detail may irritate the manager who has been oversold on the speed of computers.

There is a concurrent trap into which the zealot falls, however: He tends to overlook or minimize the time and cost required to develop and maintain a business model. Here the manager must beware, lest he find himself directed or even manipulated by the technical staff. Some systems people can learn management language quickly and convince the manager that what they propose is just a technical program, even though it may really involve changes in basic policy.

The complexity and rapid obsolescence of computer hardware is a worrisome factor to a manager. The normal reaction is, why not wait until the situation stabilizes and avoid massive commitment to Edsel or DC-3 models of hardware?

4. Managers' anti-management scientist reaction. The era when the technical and business community reacted with awe and amazement to the new computer miracle has by and large passed. Vestiges of the second era, or adolescence, still linger somewhat on occasions when euphoria envelops people with a belief that computers can cure the world's ills. When an executive learns, however, that all the calculations done at Los Alamos back in 1945, working around the clock for one year, can now be accomplished by a Dartmouth undergraduate in one afternoon while he shares the computer's time with 30 other people, he quickly loses that euphoria.

The younger scientists, not having gone through an economic depression, a world war, or a personal career cycle, are understandably restless when faced with the hindrances raised by these executives to the adoption of a systems approach to business. A few of the parvenu members of this newer generation also tend to indulge in some intellectual one-upmanship.

The current generation of management scientists belongs to the era of first maturity, where there is a realistic businesslike view, without illusion, of the prospects for this new science. Much of the "anti-reaction" of management will be eliminated as the management scientists present more practical contributions of their tools and skills. At this point in time, we need more stress on applications and less on the theory to bring this rapprochement about.

5. The value of experience and intuition. Leonardo da Vinci observed that those sciences that are not born of experience and that do not end in experience are vain and full of errors. Well-applied management science can have two effects on the variety and accuracy of the managing process: It can bring forth new concepts and techniques of managing, and it can diminish many of the inefficiencies found in complex situations, especially when it comes to hitherto unmanageable problems vis-à-vis the established order within the manager group itself. These are problems with which behavioral science may be of assistance, and it is interesting that companies sometimes succeed *in spite* of their executives.

Decision theory is based on a framework in which computers explore idealized rational decisions. Executive performance, however, deals with a spectrum, running from rational decisions at the one end to rationalized decisions at the other.

The political aspects of management offer some good examples. Politics, in its finest sense, ought to be one of the manager's serious activities, because it deals with running the show. However, political factors usually provide only a distraction from the integration process of the decision maker. The politically skilled person in an organization hints subtly at others' subconscious fears and desires and provides the rationalization of a management problem in an easy-to-accept form.

These subconscious factors—along with emotion, bias, and pure intuition—are not easily put into a business model or computer program, yet they will never go out of style. In fact, after the simulation steps are completed, the personal strategy, value system, and intuition of the chief executive must come into play as a final input to his lonely decision.

Policy making—an art—is one of the most difficult tasks of the top manager. It requires that the big picture— all the objectives, goals, and plans of the organization—

be taken into account. Brilliant intuitive ad hoc improvisation here is no substitute for well-defined policy. But after the policy has been laid down and fed into the model of the problem, and after simulation approaches have been applied to it, a flash of intuitive judgment is a very valuable ingredient to add and must not be discounted.

Closing the Managementality Gap (2)

At the beginning, it was suggested that in order to close the "managementality gap" the two groups must be put in mental lockstep in four areas: understanding of the forces at work in the social-business system, recognition of the state of the art of management theory and practice, knowledge of management science potential, and familiarity with the behavioral framework of organizations.

One key to the difference between the conceptual viewpoints of the junior and senior parties lies in the scientist's attempt to view society and business in the *abstract,* as systems and subsystems, rather than in individual, personal terms. The typical manager, on the other hand, shows the human tendency to simplify complex realities so that bad situations appear the work of faulty individuals, rather than as malfunctioning social systems. It is easier for the average executive to talk about people than about abstractions.

To think that a problem can be solved by replacing personalities is often a delusion, for no leader exists in an environmental void.

A malfunctioning social or business system usually appears to have *no* feedback mechanism, but this is seldom true. The *quality* of the feedback system is the test of the efficiency of the operational system. Feedback sometimes comes to management in a discontinuous manner. The result? So-called crises.

For instance, the system may be suffering from lack of proper input by top management. We have already stressed the contributions to be made by managers and not to be attempted by management scientists—matters of policy, philosophy, objectives and goals, and other reflections of the chief executive's character and personality that may be less rational and logical than others' inputs but nevertheless valuable.

The suggestions that follow are offered to those on both sides of the gap in our social-business system. The core of the problem concerns people—people in both areas—and their behavior within the organization. The areas needing mutual understanding can be tackled with the following six suggestions.

1. Attitude. A change of attitude is called for on the part of scientists and executives alike. Each has to *want* to close this gap, to make an effort to break down this lack of understanding. The threatening mythical image projected from opposite sides of the gap must be eliminated; the "unemotional, intellectual" scientist or "computernik" and, on the other hand, the "ostrichlike, intuitive" executive, established firmly with the power to hire, fire, and spend. Both these images are unrealistic and passé, and the executive should take the lead in fostering a proper change of attitude as part of his management responsibility.

2. Two cultures. The executive survives year in and year out by his ability to live and react continually with several "cultures": his own organization, competitors, suppliers, customers, shareowners, bankers, and the government. He juggles these all the time, exercising his intuitive and inferential reasoning powers and avoiding friction and conflicts between cultures.

The scientist, on the other hand, is reasonably aloof from such interfacial problems, avoids them generally, and does not normally consider such input into the program for attaining his objective. Yet logic and technical analysis or synthesis are seldom sufficient to achieve success in a business enterprise. The dual cultures of science and management must be combined and understood.

From the executive viewpoint, the style of managing does not always assume a logical sequence, but it has a pattern in which the manager is comfortable. (The manager may make other managers uncomfortable with this style, but that's another story!) Formality is forced upon the subordinate organization, but a "small shop" style is comfortable for the top executives because they understand each other without verbalizing full definitions. In fact, some areas of the management process are best left ambiguous. The means of obtaining the result is of minor importance unless it is intolerably costly or time-consuming.

Different relative value systems are implicit in the gap between the management scientist and the manager. The criteria for these value systems may be wrong, but the fact that they do exist side by side should be acknowledged.

Many intellectually inclined young management scientists have entered industry as a third choice. The first call is to continue in academic research; the second is to government service. Industry has, perhaps, the least attractive value system in their estimation. Some of these men tend to continue to identify themselves with a university value system of intellectual challenges, rather than with operating problems and the value systems of business. There is a great need for the successful management scientist to become committed to his company's success, not to the success of his techniques.

We must recognize that executives are committed to the corporation and are concerned primarily with groups of people and communications. They deal with relatively short-range problems such as selling products, ideas, and activities, and they are concerned with long-range business stability and survival and with the possible.

On the other hand, scientists are committed to their profession and are more concerned with things than with people. They prefer to deal with longer-range, intellectually challenging problems, with the unstabling process of change itself. They tend to seek perfection rather than what is possible.

3. Communication. Not only are scientists usually uninterested in communication, but their language differs from that of executives. For example, the old-fashioned cut-and-try approach is now called "stochastic simulation done in a policy laboratory." The two groups *must* communicate with each other, however. Executives must learn to think and speak with more comfort in the systems- and symbol-oriented world, and the management scientist must avoid the Barnum-and-binary babble that is not understandable to the executive. Why say to the president, "The ratio of required resources for one venture against total resources available is increasing quite significantly"? "You have fewer chances at bat, Mr. President," is a far more effective way of putting it.

4. Intellectual one-upmanship. This must be eliminated, since it defeats understanding. The junior party— the management scientist—sometimes tends to oversell his potential contribution to the management process, partly because he lacks knowledge of the environment and the complexities of executive decision making.

A professor in a leading business school in this country recently described the several levels of intellectual sophistication existing in schools today that have an effect on graduates who enter industry. First, he said, there are those in academia who do nothing of academic substance but who recognize their shortcomings. This group presents no problem to the graduate. Second, there are those who accomplish nothing of substance but who talk a great game about it. They can do considerable damage. Third, there are those harmless types who really do accomplish things of substance in the academic world but who are too busy to be interested in talking about their accomplishments to outsiders. Fourth, there is a group—and its members are as sharp as they come—that understands this whole system, and this is the group that gets the most attention. It exerts an unfortunate influence on younger men who may unwittingly fall into the trap of being willing to overstate the expectations of their management science approach to the management process—a practice that must be eliminated if the managementality gap is to be closed.

In academia, if you can "mislead" your colleagues by performing intellectual one-upmanship, you sometimes can gain a point to which your academic colleagues will say, "Touché!" Top management, however, doesn't appreciate this game very much.

5. *Self-management.* It was Machiavelli who argued that half of men's actions are ruled by chance and the other half are governed by the men themselves. Today, with more attention being paid to the *chance* side of the

equation, scientists must learn to manage themselves before they can expect to contribute to managing a business. This is a matter of experience, maturity, and style. The systems experts must eliminate the James Bond overtones: the war-room image, the humanized-computer threat, the zip jargon, and the ejection seat.

6. *A common mission.* Executives and management scientists must first agree on a common mission and develop a shared commitment to proceed on a course of action. The mission should be task-oriented rather than organizationally oriented, and its context must be one of longer-range objectives so that the solution will lead somewhere. It must cope with the desire of the scientist to research something intellectually challenging, possibly unrelated to problems of immediate importance to management.

At the same time, the common mission must deal with the realistic world of business and not with purely theoretical problems. The scientist is not likely to be interested in dealing in the short-range area, in spite of the fact that if he really dug into the manager's job, he would find it deeply complex and as challenging as many longer-range, more fanciful projects.

There is a recent trend in management circles to approach problems via the task-force route. In such cases, rank and hierarchical straitjackets are set aside until the task is completed, and a third party is often used as a catalyst to help close the gap. A consultant—a personnel officer, for example—may be able to perform this function if he is included in the task force. Perhaps this is a route which should be explored more fully.

With more than 8 million new managers needed in our economy by 1978, we require the full input of our present management and scientific leaders. Tomorrow's leaders, about 13 percent of all employed persons in the United States, will undoubtedly come in larger measure from the ranks of a new breed of men who are well schooled in both management and behavioral sciences.

We began this chapter by suggesting that managers take a hint from politics and rigorously analyze the consequences of their decisions first, *before* choosing one solution over the alternatives. Another lesson from politics may help close this discussion. Lord Salisbury, in Robert Blake's brilliant biography of *Disraeli,* is quoted on the subject of pursuing bad policy too long: "The commonest error in politics is sticking to the carcass of dead policies." Now is the time to debride some of our outdated management policies—that is, carefully remove those that are obsolete—and get on with a modern approach to the business challenge. To do this in business—as in all organic systems—the true need is for interaction, trust, communication, commitment, and a period of gestation in order to close the "managementality gap."

References

[1] H. Igor Ansoff and John M. Stewart, "Strategies for a Technology-Based Business," *Harvard Business Review* (Nov.–Dec. 1967), pp. 70–83.

[2] Robert Kirk Mueller, "The Managementality Gap," in *IEEE Transactions on Systems and Cybernetics,* Vol. SSC-5, No. 1 (Jan. 1969). Original publication of this manuscript after presentation at the Optimal Systems Planning Symposium, and IFAC Symposium at Cleveland, Ohio on June 21, 1968. Also, *Science Journal* (Nov. 1968), Iliffe Industrial Publications Ltd., London, and *Management Decision* (Winter 1968), Heywood-Temple Publications Ltd., London.

Additional Readings

Hans J. Love, "Operations Research as a Tool for Decision Making," *Journal of Industrial Engineering* (Sept. 1967), pp. 539–549.
Fremant E. Kast, "A Dynamic Planning Model, an Application of Systems Management to Industry," *Business Horizons* (Indiana University School of Business), Vol. 11, pp. 61–68.

PART TWO:
Survival

v. Survival of the Fittest

As long as a manager recognizes the factors that impede his progress, he can cope with them and strive better to survive. The purpose of this chapter is to characterize the undergrowth that chokes managerial careers and the selection process of the administrative jungle.

As C. Northcote Parkinson has pointed out, "It is not the business of the botanist to eradicate the weeds. Enough for him if he can tell us just how fast they grow." (1) And so, perhaps, we will be able to give some insight into this survival syndrome as it pertains to managerial careers.

There is a seeming paradox in our management system in the principle of equal opportunity and the principle of unequal rank and status. This paradox makes for a thriving, competitive, healthy management system. The second principle provides motives for the maximum use of our energies, for the orderly functioning of organizations, and for the establishment of hierarchies of responsible leaders. The manager must perceive the interaction of both principles in order to make his way in a considerate but determined manner.

Let us first review a study of more than 8,000 success-

ful business leaders as reported by W. Lloyd Warner and
James Abegglen in *Big Business Leaders in America:* (2)

> The ordered process of occupational succession in Big
> Business demonstrates that at least in this prestigeful
> and highly valued part of our economic life our society
> is somewhat more fluid and flexible than it was yester-
> day. There is more circulation in and out of the higher
> and lower statuses; more men from different family back-
> grounds enter, hold, and leave powerful positions. The
> fathers of the elite and the ambitious, striving men at
> the bottom both have greater awareness that the prin-
> ciples of birth alone are insufficient for maintaining
> high status today. Values of achieved status and social
> mobility are expressed more fully, and those of inherited
> position less so than a generation ago.

As J. W. N. Sullivan said: "For every living creature
that succeeds in getting a footing in life, there are thou-
sands or millions that perish." And this holds true in the
hierarchical realm of the large business, government, or
other institutional organization. The headhunters are
always in search of needed top executive talent to fill a
demand that seems to be insatiable, not only in the United
States, but in the expanding Western European economy
and, in fact, throughout the Free World. Only in recent
years, with the twentieth-century managerial revolution
and the constant growth and realignment of enterprises in
the increasingly competitive environment of the industrial
areas of the world, have the succession and accretion of corporate power changed from the more traditional Horatio
Alger or father-son type of method to that revealed in
the Warner-Abegglen survey.

Body Politic and Body Physiologic

Biological models of organizational growth have been demonstrated by many students of organization. Mason Haire, Ralph M. Hower, Charles D. Orth, Joseph McGuire, Walter B. Cannon, Kenneth E. Boulding, Oswald Knauth, Neil W. Chamberlin, and others have used such models to emphasize concepts of growth and stability.

The late Dr. Walter B. Cannon, George Higginson Professor of Physiology at Harvard Medical School, was perhaps the first to suggest that the automatic regulatory mechanisms of the body physiologic might be applied to the body politic. The survival of the human body, Cannon observed, is due to the body organization's functioning actively with respect to change, fatigue, and attack, both internally and externally. There exists within the body a remarkable ability to regulate the steady state of a healthy human being against internal and external factors.

Like the body, other organizations—such as a management group—face internal and external problems of adjustment. Although many sociologists and firing-line executives would discount the analogy, there is increasing justification for this comparison. The ability of industries and commerce to operate in both normal and emergency situations, calling on stored resources, is a direct parallel to bodily homeostasis.

The success of the body physiologic [Cannon observed (3)] would seem to intimate that in the body politic there should be a thorough cooperation of functional groups, with the administrative groups dependent like the others on a common welfare. And the failure of the body physiologic to survive would seem to emphasize the importance of adequate replacement of functional groups as an elemental necessity for the social body's persistence. Its firmest basis for longevity and stability would appear to be a generally accepted mode of replacement socially sponsored as being orderly and just.

But the organization expects more than survival, as Professor Dalton E. McFarland of Michigan State University has pointed out: "Organizational health, then, clearly reflects the twin goals of company survival and growth. Survival is a minimum goal, and an important one. But the healthy enterprise pours its energies into a vigorous struggle for progress, if not supremacy, in a competitive environment." (4) How well the organization adjusts and responds to the struggle of competition depends on the quality of its leadership.

Survival and Advancement

Slow-witted and heavy-footed, the brontosaurus was little more than 35 tons of dead weight. It died because it simply would not take the necessary initiative to stay alive. This kind of lagging behind can be fatal to a career in management, and only those with the initiative and ability to keep up with their business competition will survive.

A 1955 study of 3,394 elections to the presidencies of 68 professional organizations over almost a century, conducted by Harvey C. Lehman, is interesting because of its analogy to competitive management situations in the economic arena of business and industry. (5) Although prestige may be attained at any level, from the 20s to the late 80s, the study revealed that men in their 50s were most likely to be elected to the presidency of a professional organization. There was a tendency for more youthful presidents to be elected by professional groups that included a large proportion of research workers, rather than practitioners, and relatively youthful presidents tended to emerge on top of newly founded professional groups. Numerous factors appeared to enter into the pattern; sheer professional merit seemingly was not the sole factor insuring election.

Warner and Abegglen's study of the careers and backgrounds of American business leaders showed that many factors affect achievement and survival in the management scheme. (2) To paraphrase these:

- Opportunity continues to increase and to make it possible for men from all levels to move into elite positions in commerce and industry.
- The opportunity to get an advanced education is one of the most equalizing forces in our social system, and formal education is the royal road that distinguishes the leaders of large corporations from the general population. Only one-fourth of the group were not college graduates, versus about five-sixths of the general population.
- Career mobility is a common element for the mature leaders, who have made their way to the top through a variety of channels and methods. This requires certain psychological equipment in the individual, allowing constant demonstration of his adequacy and reiterated proof of his independence.
- Career mobility is enormously demanding of the

energies of able men and requires psychological and personality adjustments, and concentration on these demands affects him and his home life in terms of isolation, fatigue, and so on.

- The emotional capacity to leave both people and situations, adjust to new ones, and leave these in turn; an unconscious faith in the malleability of their world; and a firm belief in our social system are common characteristics of top business leaders.
- Brilliance is not a common factor, although the mobile elite have an intelligence substantially above average. Judgments are quick, tough, and accurate; and the men are not easily distracted.

Out of this scramble, leaders in the form of company presidents emerge. What special quality enables one to become president of a large company? In recent years there has been a popular assumption that managers with a marketing background were rising to the top of our larger organizations to an increasing extent because of the shift in competitive emphasis toward marketing opportunities and problems. But when William P. Dommermuth of the University of Texas (6) followed 248 postwar presidents of the nation's largest manufacturing firms for 16 years, he found that there was no single special background that was dominant and paved the way for these men to reach the top, although some types of specialty training helped more than others. Men from production actually led the field, followed closely by those who specialized in general management, marketing, and finance, in that order. After getting to the top, the presidents who lasted the longest were those who had specialized in general management, followed by those from finance, production, and marketing. Tenure in the jobs studied averaged a little over seven and a half years for the longest category and five and a half years for the shortest.

The short average tenures indicated in this study may be misleading, but it is certainly true that the rigors and hazards of the job of being president of a large company often reduce the years of survival at the top. The climate within an industry or a company may also shorten the president's term of office or the vigor of his leadership.

Impediments to Success

From the Greeks the behaviorists have borrowed words that we can perhaps purloin to label five factors that tend to undermine the effectiveness of today's manager. These are hazards to survival that can be detrimental to the manager's career if allowed to develop to full maturity. The five are kainotophobia, drapetomania, hypobulia, philoneism, and kakorrhaphiophobia!

1. *Kainotophobia,* or fear of change, is discussed in the chapter on behavioral basics.
2. *Drapetomania,* or an uncontrolled tendency to wander, is a sapping factor in a manager's personal planning of his career or the task at hand.
3. *Hypobulia* refers to a psychoneurotic haste in making decisions that is approached by the let's-get-things-done type of manager who eschews the plan-evaluate-assess-and-study approach. Chapter II on "Managerial Instinct" exposes some of the hazards of a tendency toward hypobulia.

4. *Philoneism* expresses the current—perhaps perennial—addiction of managers to new techniques, new tools, new theories (some good, some weak) that reach fad stage in their popular acceptance. Recent examples include brainstorming, executive aircraft, automation, corporate marriages, bigness, internationalization, and executive diets.

5. *Kakorrhaphiophobia* is an advanced stage or exaggerated degree of fear of failure; it causes indecision in thought and action. In management, this may manifest itself outwardly in such forms as ulcers, alcoholism, nervousness, fingernail biting, calorie counting, and sometimes excessive travel or overdevelopment of office accoutrements in the form of sauna baths, automobile telephones, art collections, multiple telephones and secretaries, and other paraphernalia that enhance the manager's feeling of security.

Although borrowed somewhat cavalierly from the field of psychopathology, these terms when applied to managers do express several trends in organizations and the survival of the fittest of the managerial breed. They certainly can be described as common weaknesses of the manager, and they must be recognized and dealt with by the would-be successful executive.

Natural Selection in Business

The chief scientific excitement of the nineteenth century was the Darwin theory of evolution. Darwin's conception comprised certain great principles in which he noted the interrelation of living organisms—a "web of life." He recognized the struggle for existence and the fact of variation, and he considered the mechanism of evolution to be selection through adaptation. This ability of certain living things to adapt themselves to their environment, while others fail to survive the rigors of the environment, runs the entire gamut of living organisms and is certainly evident in man, in both his early evolutionary stages and his more advanced state in today's complicated world.

Adolph Hitler adopted a more violent version of survival in support of his *völkisch* concept, as stated in *Mein Kampf*. (7) He postulated an unequal original status of certain peoples:

> The *völkisch* concept of the world recognizes that the primordial racial elements are of the greatest significance to mankind—we cannot admit that one race is equal to another. By recognizing that they are different, the *völkisch* concept separates mankind into races of superior and inferior quality. On the basis of this recognition it feels bound, in conformity with the eternal will that dominates the universe, to postulate the victory of the better and the stronger and the subordination of the inferior and weaker. And so it pays homage to the truth that the principle underlying all Nature's operations is the aristocratic principle, and it believes that this law holds good even down to the last individual organism. . . .

This alleged relative superiority of some individuals is sometimes a factor in the business struggle (see Chapter XI on "The Resonance Factor"). Hitlerian methods and concepts, however, have no place in the ethical, social-minded arena of today's competitive economic organizations. Certain managers may appear to have a starting edge on others climbing the management ladder, but the redeeming feature in the majority of companies that survive competitively is that they must depend on the most capable managerial talent as a means of organizational preservation. In most firms, there is a constant movement of talent at all levels owing to the organizational demand for good managers, which always outpaces the supply. Training programs, appraisal systems, performance reviews, compensation practices, the proselyting of competitors, stockholder reactions—all tend to ease out the less fit at the various levels of management.

Over a few years' time, the free enterprise system has a way of causing the most able managers to emerge at leadership levels in an organization and to stay there or move on up—if the scoreboard on corporate growth and profits supports their tenure of office. When a company is continually in trouble, and after all the obvious improvements have been made in production, marketing, and the other functional areas, there must inevitably be a change of management in an effort to seek leadership that can cope with the obstacles faced.

The web of life that exists in a management organization with its interrelationships of people and functions is one in which there is a continual shifting of leadership roles. This is due to the failure of certain managers to adapt to the competition from other would-be managers about them in their personal struggles for power and position in the company.

A manager usually has at least 30 years of responsible management time, assuming that he enters management ranks at 35 years of age and retires at 65. This 30-year period of competing with his colleagues for prominent places in the power structure of a modern organization gives a manager at least a half-dozen levels or spheres of interest in which to test his fitness; that is, a half-dozen situations in which his ability to adapt to the competitive scene is necessary for advancement to the next career assignment. During this period, there may for many reasons—including a maturing of the individual's ideas and goals in life, his family obligations, or other factors—be a change in his willingness to adapt to a new environment, with the attendant sacrifices that always accompany increased responsibility. Thus his survival or adaptation level may be, not necessarily the top spot, but one having a degree of authority and responsibility with which he is comfortable and competitive and which suits his aims in life. All in all, the selection process in management organization is a natural one that has many parallels to Darwin's principles.

Paradox and Dichotomy in the Administrative Jungle

We come back to the paradox that modern managers face in the form of the democratic principle of equal opportunity versus the principle of unequal rank and status.

The ability to reach a relatively high rank or status seldom is totally within the control of the individual manager. The best potential performer may not be called upon, or he may not uncover an opportunity to perform in his best style or to the fullest extent of his capabilities. When there are several candidates for a responsible position, only one can be chosen; and the factors of seniority, nepotism, demands outside the classical qualifications, adverse timing, or just plain "traditional" methods of selection may affect the organizational level at which a manager finds himself. The needs of the organization may be such that one manager can adequately fill a key job even though there are others with equal or perhaps greater talents.

Nevertheless, final success or failure is very seldom a random occurrence, for luck and chance do not really determine career achievement or survival in the long run. The workings of social and economic laws ultimately bring organizational success or failure and certainly are the criteria for individual managerial survival.

Each individual manager must determine for himself what is right and just for those he supervises. The paradox of equal opportunity with unequal rank and status is inherent in our system. A major part of the manager's assignment in the economic scheme of things is to lower costs of service and production, and these include human costs. Not many of our research and technical staffs are engaged in making jobs more satisfying from the standpoint of the manager or the employee, compared with those engaged in reducing money costs.

In our system, where business is largely controlled by shareholders who indirectly determine the course of the business, the danger is always present that there will be little concern for the people involved. It is up to management to accept this responsibility.

Newsweek magazine (8) has pointed out that the diverse demands burdening today's managers call for "every bit of the polished versatility attributed to the fifteenth-century Renaissance Man. In its finest form, the art of top management today is practiced by a kind of Renaissance Executive—a man who blends business leadership with extracurricular breadth and tempers the profit motive with a social conscience."

The manager thus finds himself torn on the one hand with the demands of remaining competitive and, on the other, with the delicate problem of doing so with people and without unfairly expending human effort. To handle this dual responsibility is the challenge of those who would survive in the administrative jungle.

References

[1] C. Northcote Parkinson, *Parkinson's Law and Other Studies in Administration* (Boston: Houghton Mifflin Co., 1957), p. 13.

[2] W. Lloyd Warner and James Abegglen, *Big Business Leaders in America* (New York: Harper & Bros., 1955), p. 200.

[3] Walter B. Cannon, "AAAS Presidential Address," *Science* (1941).

[4] Dalton E. McFarland, "Organizational Health and Company Efficiency," *Business Topics* (Summer 1965), p. 46.

[5] Harvey C. Lehman, "Ages at Time of First Election of Presidents of Professional Organizations," *The Scientific Monthly* (May 1955), pp. 293–298.

[6] William P. Dommermuth, "On the Odds of Becoming Company President," *Harvard Business Review* (May–June 1966), pp. 65–72.

[7] Adolph Hitler, *Mein Kampf*, unexpurgated edition translated by James Murphy (London: Hurst & Blockett, Ltd., 1939), pp. 28–29.

[8] "Renaissance Executive," *Newsweek* (Nov. 18, 1963).

The ultimate source of executive authority is organized society. It is an extension of the right of private property. It is received ultimately by delegation from organized society, through ownership, to the executive who is responsible for the management of the business organization and its operations.

—RALPH CURRIER DAVIS

VI. Executive Authority

IN ancient Greece, a custom prevailed for a time which required a man proposing a law in the popular assembly to do so on a platform with a rope around his neck. If his law passed, they removed the rope; if it failed, they removed the platform. Similarly, in early American Indian tribes, the man who dared represent himself as a rainmaker lived a go/no-go existence. If the rainmaker's prognostications failed to achieve at least reasonable accuracy, he was buried alive. The executive today runs the same sort of risk in maintaining his position, and it is likely that opinion rather than events will unseat him in times of trouble.

The problem of dealing with property, both tangible and intangible, has always been a vital one as man evolved and organized his societies through the centuries. Various cultures, consisting of the knowledge, beliefs, morals, laws, customs, art, and other products of the capabilities and habits of human beings, evolved mainly through heredity, environment, and the interactions of people with each other. Lord Raglan, author and anthropologist, calls culture "roughly, everything we do and the monkeys don't." In this sense, culture concerns what people do to and with each other, and it pertains to matters of agreement, obligation, trust, and service that bear on the function of organizational management.

Unfortunately, in a democracy the free enterprise organization has a schizoid personality. It must deal with the economic responsibility of the enterprise to society and economic survival of the enterprise and, at the same time, protect the interests of the "governed" member of the enterprise. The divorce of enterprise ownership and control presents additional problems, since realistic control is in the hands of hired hands—that is, managers— and the legal ownership of the corporate property resides in widely held stockholders' portfolios.

Peter F. Drucker (1) makes the point that an enterprise is by nature a governmental institution, and, as a governing body, it must rule in the interests of its subjects —meaning its employees and owners—if it is to be a legitimate "government." The first concern of the enterprise is the production of goods or services that will meet a need at a price that is the same as (or less than) the price prevailing elsewhere, leaving a margin of profit for the investor, for growth, for expansion, and for surplus. The purpose of business is in fact to make such goods or render such services to society, and in order to be permanently successful the enterprise must be of ever increasing value to society.

It seems that Professor Drucker's basic question as to whether management can be legitimate under these conditions is answerable in the affirmative—if a long enough time frame of reference is used and if management assumes a professional role in keeping a proper balance among the contending forces affecting the enterprise. A professional manager will accept in total the social responsibility of business while protecting the interests of his constituents: owners, other managers, employees, consumers, vendors, the community, and the public at large.

The concept of professionalism in management requires the manager to act as a trustee for the whole of society in order to preserve his position in our free enterprise system. In acting as a trustee he is carrying out a legitimate activity.

What Is Management?

Management is struggling to attain the status of a profession and has made remarkable progress in the relatively short period of time since 1903 when Frederick W. Taylor published *Shop Management* for those interested in the management of industrial enterprises. With only two-thirds of a century of readily accessible modern literature on the subject of management as it applies to our highly developed industrial societies, it is no wonder that the values and ethics involved in the practice of management have yet to "wait a hundred generations" to have their legitimacy confirmed by posterity.

There has even been difficulty in getting a generally accepted definition of what management is. Lawrence A. Appley, chairman of the board of the American Management Association, who has undoubtedly done more than any other single person to clarify and identify the activity in which managers engage, cites two definitions. The first, disseminated by the Training Within Industry Division of the War Manpower Commission during World War II, is simply that "management is getting things done through other people." The second was developed in 1940 when business executives and business school professors met at the Schenley Hotel in Pittsburgh for the purpose of developing a definition of management. They arrived at the following: "Management is guiding human and physical resources into dynamic organization units which attain their objectives to the satisfaction of those served and with a high degree of morale and sense of attainment on the part of those rendering the service." Mr. Appley has expanded on this further: "Management is an activity unlike any other activity. It requires certain qualifications, certain preparation, certain skills, certain attitudes, and knowledge of the use of certain tools. Management is a profession. It's an activity that gets things done through other people, and it calls for the skills and capabilities to guide human and physical resources to successful attainment with great satisfaction and rewards."

Because management is such a broad concept, and because its activities are so bound up in an ever changing society with ever changing values and ethics, there is no simple law that brands the management function as a single clearly defined legitimate activity. Today's manager must demonstrate the legitimacy of the management function by professional conduct in his trustee and leadership roles. This he must do through recognition of his total public responsibilities as trustee for the interests of society as a whole, not exclusively for the interests of the stockholders.

Management's Agreements and Obligations

Business managers, by virtue of their appointment, their work, and their organizational situation, have multiple interfaces with other groups. To repeat: These include their subordinates, their associates, investors, vendors, customers, competitors, the community, and the public at large. There are tacit agreements and obligations inherent in our social system that form a grid of formal and informal agreements with and obligations to these groups. Some of these agreements and obligations are derived from the concept of trust, some from property rights, others from legal order, and still others from generally sanctioned principles of authority.

The manager's activities in common with associates and subordinates hinge on agreements having to do with psychological matters, such as the exchange of mutual trust for mutual security and the submerging of individual interests in group interests. These are not legal matters; rather, they are matters of morals, values, and ethics, and their sanction is derived from centuries of societal and cultural evolution.

From the same roots is derived the manager's recognition of his responsibility to the community and the public. The government charters a corporation and gives it perpetual life as an instrument for accomplishing certain economic objectives in our system. The managers chosen by the owners of the corporations are given certain rights and powers to carry out these objectives, but the laws creating this form of organized endeavor set forth only a minor part of the legitimate function of management.

Management's agreements with vendors and customers

tend to be spelled out in written legal documents. This is normal practice in commerce and industry, and the legal framework for these relationships is fairly well established.

The manager's agreement with the owners of the business—the stockholders—is formal, legal, but indirect. The obligation of the manager to "maintain the wealth" of the owners by earning a reasonable return through his care of the property granted him in the form of an investment is well recognized legally; the power of granting or withdrawing authority and position from management resides by law in the hands of the stockholders. There is, however, a fictional aspect to the power of the stockholder in a large publicly owned corporation; instances of stockholder influence on management activities are relatively rare.

Labor–Management Rights

Perhaps no other source of intergroup conflict has caused more tension and more affected our modern social order than the tug-of-war between labor and management. Everyone also seems to have ideas and opinions on collective bargaining, the right to work, the union's power role in society, the antitrust immunity of organized labor, and the power balance in the free enterprise system.

Collective bargaining is essentially a process in which decisions of management (acting for the owners) are challenged by the unions (acting for the employees). Whether the challenges are lawful is one matter; whether they are wise is another. The unions' challenge to managerial authority is seen by some as a threat to our capitalistic system and the foundations of our competitive economy. Actually, both labor and management must chart their collective and individual courses with the common objective of maintaining a free society.

There is an unsettling judicial trend on the part of the courts to intervene in what are essentially private affairs. If management cannot perform its necessary functions, or if unions preclude it from doing so by restrictive agreements, the state will surely step in to perform those functions. Wherever in the world this has happened, whether in the past or in recent times, the lights of free enterprise, free labor, and free management have been extinguished.

The heart of the conflict between labor and management is the theory of the reserved rights of management. This doctrine is the basic frame of reference for collective bargaining agreements. Management's authority is supreme in all matters except those it has expressly conceded in the labor contract, or those in which its authority is restricted by law. Management looks to its legal agreements with unions to find out which of its rights and powers are either shared with the union or conceded outright.

The doctrine of implied obligations is a corollary to the reserved-rights theory of management. This doctrine acknowledges employee benefits whenever a contract is open for negotiations but not between those periods when negotiations are officially in progress.

These two doctrines allow labor arbitration to proceed in the United States in a pragmatic way that has wide acceptance. The ideologic conflicts outside the contract terms are resolvable—provided there is recognition of management's inherent right to manage, as trustees, the property given them by the owners—as long as the operation accepts a responsibility to society as a whole to preserve the free enterprise system.

The Trust Concept—Property Rights

In an industrial democracy, organized society is the source of most sanctions for the operation of a business. Private enterprise receives its primary sanction through the right of private property—that is, the right of individuals to hold and use property for their personal benefit, with due regard for the private-property rights of others.

When the state acquires complete control of property, it makes little difference who holds title to it. An individual's freedom of action and his future destiny depend in a great measure on his right of private property. Article V of the Constitution of the United States reads, "No person shall be . . . deprived of life, liberty, or property without due process of law; nor shall private property be taken for public use without just compensation."

The protection of private-property rights is the basis of one of management's obligations. The source of executive authority is a society of multiple owners, and this in part is an extension of the concept of the right of private property. This right is received by delegation from organized society through its laws concerning ownership, which in the case of the executive responsible for the enterprise's management places him in a legal trusteeship and anoints him with a formal legitimacy in matters concerning the organization and its operations.

Professional Management as an Answer

The best thing managers can do to demonstrate the legitimacy of their activities is to respond to the call to accept broader social responsibility in our free enterprise system. Only by overt acceptance of a leadership role in the whole society will the manager receive the more explicit legal rights or sanction to execute his function.

The concept of professionalism instills in the manager a will to discharge his functions and be faithful to his trust. With the recognition that his trust is extended to him by society as a whole, he responds to the interests of all concerned and his practice of management is definitely affected. The late Edgar Monsanto Queeny (2) put it this way: "Managements respond to public opinion. Out of a public opinion that places high values on the social consciousness of business will arise an era of cleansed and purged private enterprise which can attain any social objective."

In order for public opinion to accept professionalism in management, a certain validation of the qualifications and preparation of managers is required. This includes educational certification, an internship, legal recognition of suitability to practice, and an ethical code for management. In addition there must be a dedication to service, a recognized competence in something a layman cannot do for himself, and some sort of mechanism for disciplinary review of continuing qualifications to serve. The notion of public responsibility should be paramount in the concept of professionalism.

When management attains a professional status, it will

be through broad public acceptance rather than a mere legal order. The manager's sense of legitimacy will come from the feelings and value judgments of the people. Only in this way will he gain the support of society as a whole.

References

[1] Peter F. Drucker, *The New Society* (New York: Harper & Bros., 1949), Chapter 10.

[2] Edgar M. Queeny, *The Spirit of Enterprise* (New York: Charles Scribner's Sons, 1943).

Additional Readings

Douglas McGregor, *The Professional Manager* (New York: Mc-Graw-Hill Book Co., 1967).

Robert L. Peabody, *Organizational Authority: Superior-Subordinate Relationships in Three Public Service Organizations* (New York: Atherton Press, 1964).

Heinz Hartmann, *Authority and Organization in German Management* (Princeton: Princeton University Press, 1959).

Frederick H. Harbison and Charles A. Myers, *Management in the Industrial World* (New York: McGraw-Hill Book Co., 1959).

J. M. Juran, "Management Prerogatives and Rights in the Job," *Machine Shop Magazine* (April 1950).

Larry R. Heath, "Labor Management Problems," *Virginia Law Review* (Mar. 1964).

Paul Prasow and Edward Peters, "New Perspectives on Management's Reserved Rights," *Labor Law Journal* (Jan. 1967), pp. 3–14.

Ralph Currier Davis, *The Fundamentals of Top Management* (New York: Harper & Bros., 1951).

VII. The Catalyst: Profit

SOMEONE once said that "business is what, if you don't do it, you have to go out of." As we have seen, a private enterprise activity dies unless the business continually justifies its existence by performing a service or manufacturing a product useful to and desired by people—fulfilling a need while the company is deriving a profit.

Most businessmen consider it their first responsibility to see that their company makes a profit. The responsibility doesn't start or end there, for no company exists or operates in a sequestered environment consisting of itself, its customers, and its suppliers. A business is part of the social system, and the manager is partly responsible for its continuity. Yet profit is necessary for survival of the business, and weakening or destroying its ability to make an adequate profit will soon adversely affect the mainstream of society's system.

Profit is the catalyst that stimulates management to accept business risks. Since business is the function of serving human needs at a profit, the profit is not only an ideal in itself but a necessity to an advancing democratic social order. All business enterprises, particularly large economic units, can stimulate or depress the economic sectors of our nation, which in turn affect the other sectors and, in fact, the entire social system.

Profit also serves an important regulating function. As another authority has said, it acts like a traffic cop, directing the use of resources into the places where production can flow most freely. The consumer decides what he wants, not the business manager, and only if the manager correctly appraises the consumer's needs and wants can he profit. The business manager must be profit-minded, in short, if we as a nation are to make the most efficient use of our resources. Without the catalyst of profit, there is no incentive for the efficient use of people, technology, time, money, and materials.

Money Profit Is Not the Only Profit

Achievement is measured by what it is worth in money terms. According to capitalist theory, man is motivated by the so-called profit motive.

In the *Communist Manifesto*, Marx and Engels held that the intrinsic or nonmonetary worth of any activity tended to be destroyed with growing specialization, such as the factory system in the economy. In Communist or Socialist countries, production for profit is therefore abolished in favor of production for use. Some small rays of hopeful change that have appeared recently seem to recognize profit making as a motivating force of value to their social system; however, the world of the capitalist and entrepreneur is still on this side of the iron and bamboo curtains.

The measure of achievement for capitalist businessmen is certainly paced by money—at least, in the first instance, as a symbol of achievement. But the need for achievement is much broader than the need for monetary compensation. Generalized achievement goals are certainly catalysts in their own right, whether they be higher standards of living, greater status and prestige, extension of the free enterprise system, the conquest of nature, or the eradication of disease, poverty, and ignorance. There is ample evidence that it is not profit per se that makes the businessman tick, but a strong desire to do a good job. (1)

Managers as Trustees

The place of profit in a management philosophy must be considered in relation to the other specifications of that philosophy. If management is the intellect that controls and effectively uses human and physical resources to achieve the objectives of the enterprise, it has a trusteeship role. Usually the owners of an enterprise select a management to conduct the business and thus assign it a trusteeship that, in addition to involving loyalty to the owners, involves a moral obligation to perform efficiently and successfully. Success is usually interpreted in terms of reasonable profit for the owners, fair remuneration for labor, and a nest egg of profit set aside to perpetuate the business. Corporate enterprise has perpetual life, so the overall concept of an objective must ideally be immortal. Charters change and objectives change, of course, but in a theoretical sense the goal is to produce and/or sell goods or services on terms that will contribute to the survival and growth of the organization.

There is nothing in this philosophy to suggest that an organization aims to achieve maximum excess revenue or

profit. The term "maximum profit" is meaningless unless
the time period is specified. The purpose of a business is to
serve customers and, in doing so, to generate profit for
continued support and stimulation of the business. This
purpose may differ from the purpose of those who contribute labor or financial resources; their purpose is usually to earn a worthwhile and even maximum income for
themselves. But the result of a successful business is to provide this increasing return to those who labor in it or
supply its finances.

Sumner Slichter (2) pointed out 40 years ago that the
two principal functions of profits are (*a*) bringing about
the distribution of production among different industries
in accordance with the demand for it and (*b*) stimulating
management efficiency. The stimulation to the manager-
owner of the small enterprise is greatest because he receives all the profit. Slichter suggests that, in the case of
large enterprises that are not owner-managed, the stimulation seems to come from fear of loss of profit and thus
jeopardy for the managers' positions.

Profit Is a Good Six-Letter Word

Historically, business and profit have been targets for
criticism by the public, the clergy, the government, and
the academicians from the time when the Greeks blurred
the line between thieves and merchants by making Hermes
the god of both. With time and intellectual breakthroughs,
some of the ancient hostilities have withered, and the role
of the businessman in society has increased in stature—
at least until relatively recent times when its values are
again being questioned in certain sectors.

The disinterest in business careers currently being evinced by students is causing many inquiries and many proposals for advancing the understanding of the role of business in a free society. Federal government recognition of this role is evidenced by the encouragement given to business's efforts in attacking major social problems: improvement of poverty-stricken areas, aid to developing nations, easing of racial tensions, urban renewal, and so on.

The concept of profit as a selfish hoard to be withdrawn from society, never to be disturbed, is outmoded. Profit is immediately put to work as a further investment in the modernization and continuing growth of business. As Motorola's chairman of the board, Robert W. Galvin, states it, "The equation between profit and the attainment of social goals is immediate, continuous, and inseparable."

Polls show that about half the people in our country think that business is making too much profit. Two-thirds of the people think that, although money spent on new equipment and machinery does increase output, the owners get most of the benefit of the increased production. No wonder that profit has an unsavory public relations image, if the public is so ill-informed about its amount, nature, and function. Fred C. Foy, chairman of Koppers Company, maintains that the public must be re-educated to the rightful role of profit in a free-enterprise system and to "the irreplaceable, elemental fact that profits are the spark plugs, without which our fabulous economic engine will not turn a wheel." (3)

When businessmen see their profits turning downward, they tend to cut back rather than expand their businesses, and expansion begins in earnest only when higher profit rates are in prospect. The creative power of profit is the fundamental motivating force that makes possible the economic progress that characterizes the free enterprise system.

The drive of the business manager in search of profit contributes to the material progress and prosperity of society, and this has a favorable social effect, if not a direct social purpose, in the achievement of ever higher standards of living. For this reason, the profit motive that guides the manager deserves the support of society, not its censure.

Management Is the Key

There is a growing conviction that the corporate profits of the future will depend more and more on management and managers and less and less on technology, labor, money, and natural resources. The increasing importance of the manager is reflected in the higher expenditures for the recruiting and development of executives.

With the increasing demand for better managers to guide the enterprise in producing and selling goods and services while generating a profit, it is obvious that a manager must develop his own understanding of profit as a catalyst in the free enterprise system. The quest for profits stimulates certain actions, among which the following are prominent:

1. It necessitates continual improvement in the efficiency with which the business is managed, so that profits can be improved by keeping costs down.

2. It encourages the search for improvements in products or for entirely new products to serve consumer needs, in order to create new profits to perpetuate the enterprise.
3. It provides an incentive for developing new techniques and more profitable means of distributing products and services, thus expanding the enterprise's contribution to a better standard of living.
4. It motivates the development of new markets for products through the concept of concentric technology—the use of the same technology to serve entirely different markets—thus expanding the opportunity for profit.
5. It allocates time, people, money, and natural resources to those businesses in society that best serve the needs of society, since they will provide more profitable outlets for products and services in a free society.
6. It attracts enterprise to those large social-problem areas that are identified by the government as in need of improvement in order to protect and enhance our society. This is a longer-range profit target for the private businessman, but it is nonetheless attractive to those who see the corporation as a continuing enterprise.

In fact, it is *the trend away from profit orientation* that concerns thoughtful government and business leaders who are facing up to the mounting social problems of the world today. General James M. Gavin (4), board chairman of Arthur D. Little, Inc., has told faculty members and students at Harvard University of his concern about

. . . the growing enchantment with the nonprofit approach. One gets the impression that many people believe that nonprofit is good and profit is bad. I do not intend to criticize any particular nonprofit institution, but I would like to say—based upon a number of years' association with many so-called nonprofit groups—that it has been my impression that they very often have spacious offices, wall-to-wall carpeting, more than adequate administrative help, staff sedans, and an excess of warm bodies standing about that hopefully may be gainfully employed.

This may seem to many to be a somewhat unfair picture; I know that in specific situations it is. But I know, too, that a well-managed profit-making business corporation must manage its resources very well, must think in terms of decisions to be made and results to be achieved based upon an investment of money, material, and human resources, must earn an adequate profit, and must pay a tax—municipal, state, and federal. These conditions characterize an operation in which there is a never-ending search for excellence in management, and a competitive view of others who are seeking to achieve better performance.

Of course, nonprofit organizations can be managed well, but the motivation of the manager in such a setup depends on either instinct or habit patterns rather than on an incentive as simple as financial gain, which must be the goal of managers in the business world.

Profitable Service or Production of Goods

It is a basic philosophical fact that people with a sense of investing themselves, people who know that their management regards them as investors of their business careers, will produce better products, render better customer service, and give fuller measure of value to the public than people who are merely working to earn a living.

—CHARLES G. MORTIMER

It is the executive's responsibility to provide for the continued profitable growth of an enterprise, but the help of the entire staff is needed and each employee must be motivated in this direction. Unless there is strong managerial leadership and communication of this goal of profitable growth in business, the specter of "Buridan's ass" will appear at the doorstep of the enterprise. This fourteenth-century donkey was, of course, the unfortunate animal—a fallout from Jean Buridan's theory of nominalism—which starved to death midway between two exactly similar bundles of hay because he could not decide which to choose. The manager has to define his goals and communicate them to his employees, so that they will know which bundle of hay is the one to select for the good of the enterprise.

A responsible manager's code of ethics, his religion, and his sense of social responsibility cause him to think beyond profit to the good of society. But his concepts cannot be so lofty that he forgets about the basic necessity of working for profit. That is what keeps the corporation in business.

Performing a service or producing a product for others with the objective of making a profit is a respectable goal. The profit key unlocks the drive and resources of the manager and catalyzes his action, which is beneficial to others as well as to himself. Without the catalyst of profit, the reaction has a hard time getting started, much less completed, because of the many diversionary goals and conflicts of interest that surround this activity of keeping the economic engine under power and on the right track.

References

[1] David C. McClelland, *The Achieving Society* (Princeton: D. Van Nostrand Co., Inc., 1961).

[2] Sumner Slichter, *Modern Economic Society* (New York: Henry Holt & Co., 1928), pp. 719–720.

[3] Fred C. Foy, Address Before 55th Annual Meeting of the National Industrial League in Pittsburgh, Pa. (1963). Also *News Front* (Jan. 1963), p. 46.

[4] General James M. Gavin (Ret.), *Harvard Business School Executive Letter* (July 1967).

Additional Readings

Charles G. Mortimer, McKinsey Foundation Lecture (1965).

Marvin Bower, *The Will to Manage: Corporate Success through Programmed Management* (New York: McGraw-Hill Book Co., 1966).

Clarence C. Walton, "Critics of Business: Stonethrowers and Gravediggers," *Columbia Journal of World Business* (Fall 1966), pp. 25–37.

VIII. The Social Profile

CRITICISM is a sign of recognition, though it may be a dubious honor. Because business is so important to the free enterprise fabric, the corporate behavior of managers is subject to close and constant scrutiny by educators, governmental regulatory agencies, lawmakers, labor leaders, and the voters at large.

It is well accepted that executives themselves set the moral tone of their enterprise. This is expressed in many forms of business behavior: corporate advertising, employee relations, packaging and labeling, corporate giving programs, executive compensation and expense accounts, equal opportunity policies, and most of the other external evidences of a corporation's manners in the society in which it operates.

Business must accept its measure of responsibility toward the larger framework of society in which the free enterprise endeavor is contained. The business system is essentially a customer-oriented system that is limited in comparison with other institutions of our society—the schools, government, the church, the military, and the general social system. The authority of managers to act is derived from the company's customers and from the

123

owners of the business. To serve these dual masters presents the manager with a complicated challenge, for in a
given time period the interests of the owners and those of
the customers may appear to be separate.

Profit stimulates managers to do things in the self-interest of the enterprise that are not necessarily either
beneficial or harmful to the community in which they
operate. Much of the regulation of industry by government has as its aim that of making institutions for private
profit work within policies that are beneficial to the community and making it unprofitable for them to pursue
policies that are harmful to the community. But regulations set forth by law are not enough; there must be
reliance on ethical and professional standards as well.

The necessarily partisan position of a business owner,
or a business manager employed by the owners, is due to
his being of only one economic class. The present organization of industry, in which management is primarily
responsible to the property owners rather than equally to
wage earners, consumers, and the public at large, presents
a conflict in objectives, since by assignment the managers
are partisan to the one economic class rather than all
economic classes.

The manager must face this divided responsibility
squarely and serve alike his customer master, his owner
master, and the ever present public master that accepts
and nurtures his profit system in the greater society of
which it is a part.

Business and National Purpose

From ancient Greece, Rome, Israel, China, and India
and other great societies, the works of educators, philoso-

phers, poets, artists, and religious prophets have come down to us, but not the names of many revered businessmen. Nearly 4,000 years ago, about 2000 B.C., the Code of Hammurabi was established by the sixth king of the West Semitic dynasty of Babylon. His dynasty was one of the most far-reaching governments of ancient history, the political and intellectual center of Western Asia. The code, devised by this merchant king to encourage, protect, and guide businessmen, included more than 300 laws promulgated for use in the courts of the empire. The fourth law concerned the social responsibility of a businessman or, in this instance, a businesswoman: "If outlaws hatch a conspiracy in the house of a wineseller and she does not arrest these outlaws and bring them to the palace, that wineseller shall be put to death." (1)

This forthright statement of one of the businessman's responsibilities to the national purpose springs from the realization that competition is neither a certain nor a consistently satisfactory regulator of the business system. Trade association activity has been encouraged as a corrective to this situation. Also, there has developed a more professional attitude toward obviating the necessity of formal governmental control. This professional attitude is the recognition that business and the national purpose must both be served. Profit making is not an end in itself; it is only a means of providing livelihood, and managers seeking a profit must formally accept their share of social responsibility in directing the process.

The philosophical argument for the basic value of civilization and of education rests not only on the spiritual goods created, the consciousness of finer possibilities of life, and the development of the capacities and dignity of man; their value today also lies in a better standard of living, which means a greater abundance of the material goods provided by business. "No great society has had a primitive economy," states Herbert J. Muller, professor of English and government at Indiana University. (2) When the Industrial Revolution came about, with the expansion of industry and business, economic interests became primary and for a time were regarded as ends in themselves, rather than as means to an end. It was Andrew Carnegie who sounded the clarion call to all businessmen to accept social responsibility when he argued his principle of "moral trusteeship": Men who have demonstrated ability by making a fortune are morally obligated to engage in large-scale philanthropy to return the debt they owe to society.

Down through the years, since Andrew Carnegie first proclaimed moral trusteeship, there have been opposing views on the extent of this dual responsibility of business to itself and to the national purpose. In 1964, the National Industrial Conference Board held a panel discussion on "Company Social Responsibility—Too Much or Not Enough?" (3) The opposite ends of the opinion spectrum were expressed by two businessmen. Arnold H. Maremont said: "The corporation is a statutory privilege that allows folks with savings to invest money for profit with a limited liability. The corporation is a legal entity, not a person. It is a property right, not a human right. It has no conscience." In opposition to this business-should-mind-its-own-business school, J. Irwin Miller said: "In our desire for a free society . . . we begin to find the reason for the social responsibility of a corporation. . . . For its freedom, for the maximum pursuit of its own true property interests, the corporation, like the individual, must make a free response to the society of its time."

Since the time of that panel, more than a thousand corporate executives have been queried on the question of social responsibility and about national issues of corporate concern. In the latter category, as would be expected, labor-management relationships led the way, followed by international problems, the balance of payments, inflation, government control, antitrust, patents, and consumer-protection matters. Strong emphasis was placed on issues that were business-oriented: taxes, fiscal policy, education, and problems having to do with the environment and with health.

More than 50 percent of the executives were in favor of business's taking the initiative to help solve the socio-economic issues that were listed as a result of the survey. These included Medicare, urban renewal, crime prevention, environmental control, minority-group problems, and education. Specifically, 74 percent of the executives reported that they would be willing to take the initiative in solving the problem of reduction and control of air pollution, and 73 percent expressed a willingness to help solve the problem of retraining workers left unemployed by automation.

Dr. John W. Riley sums up the results of this recent appraisal as follows: "If, indeed, American business—as many have alleged—ever did exist in a state of splendid and arrogant isolation from the larger community, those days have long since passed. I take it to be almost axiomatic that American businessmen not only have a great need to know about the changing social environment within which they operate but that, in addition, they are required to act upon this knowledge if they are to meet the minimum expectations the public has of them." (4)

Why Are We in Business?

About 500 industrial leaders from 60 Free World countries were asked by NICB why they were in business. The range of answers was extensive, with heavy overtones of the broad social responsibility of business. The simple philosophy of being in business to make a profit found little support among these international businessmen, if profit is considered an end in itself or the primary reason for being in business. In summary, these were the reasons given:

- *To make a profit.* The classical reasons: to survive, to make money for the investors, to make the business successful in order to discharge obligations to the public, and so on.
- *To provide personal satisfaction.* After the primary need for earning a living is met, enjoyment and satisfaction rank high as motives for being in business.
- *To provide work.* Foreign firms see a real obligation in a free world to provide work, in some cases as a primary aim of the enterprise. Spending money on research and development was considered as effort to expand opportunities for work.
- *To perform a service; to satisfy a need.* Services and products provide help to improve the lives of people and nations as a whole. Providing public service through company measures to improve the community also was cited.
- *To fulfill social responsibilities.* This was an important *raison d'être* among the 60 national busi-

ness groups. One went so far as to suggest that the long-range goal of business was the advancement of civilization.

- *To promote the national interest.* Some groups gave examples of companies that lost money on government work in order to carry out their responsibility toward the support of national programs of education and defense.
- *To forward democracy.* Business projects in developing countries were acknowledged to be efforts to forward the democratic system through education of people in business endeavor and extension of the free enterprise system.

The replies of these industrial leaders underline the importance of a definite social profile for a manager if he is to be effective and acceptable in his function. (5)

The Ethics of American Business

Ethics, or moral philosophy, concerns itself with judgments of approval or disapproval, rightness and wrongness, goodness or badness, virtue or vice, and the desirability of actions, dispositions, ends, objects, or states of affairs. In business, ethics concerns itself with the explanatory analysis, from a sociological or psychological standpoint, of the businessman's actions and judgments. In a more positive vein, ethics concerns the establishment of guidelines for action or ways of corporate life which will comprise a standard of conduct or *summum bonum*—that is, some ethical criteria or first principles.

"Ethics" as a word repels some people because they

tend to think of it as somehow applying to religion and philosophy and, certainly, as being out of place in the bustle of business life. Actually, however, business ethics comprises all that has been found satisfactory as a way of doing business. Acts that are covered by legal codes are included, as well as acts that are in the shadowland of unenforceable behavior. Ethics codifies in an outward way the inward sensation of rightness we feel about our business relationships with others.

There are a few people who still believe that ethical codes are necessary for the professions but have no place in business. However, the growth of professional management and the increasing importance of its role in a highly developed business complex in society dissipates the last argument against the recognition of ethics as being equally applicable to business. Whether business is a profession or not can be argued, but the general acceptance of management as a profession is growing rapidly. This places on management the responsibility of creating and following a code of ethics for its way of life that will have the austerity of self-imposition. Such a code must be potent enough to have an elevating and ennobling effect on managers whose personal standards of conduct are lower.

The Business Ethics Advisory Council in the United States said in 1962: "There is no intrinsic difference between business ethics and ethics in general. The moral standards that should govern man's behavior ought to apply to his actions in business." Today's managers are more concerned about social responsibility and business ethics than their predecessors, and this concern is not altogether altruistic. Business managers are acting in their own long-term self-interest when they adopt ethical practices and take note of what society demands of them. Regardless of the cost, business must consider and accept public values, lest it provoke the state to assert itself in laws and domination.

Business can serve society better than alternative systems, and managers are awakening to the full implications of this statement. The power possessed by managers must be used cautiously and with society's interest as well as profit maximization in mind. Professional managers know, in an old phrase, that the first duty of a noble is nobility, and that *noblesse oblige* is as appropriate a motto for the professional managerial elite as it was for the French patrician class.

The collective support obtained by businessmen who band together in trade associations in a voluntary effort to standardize practices at a high level has given impetus to ethical codes for various industries, and these codes are constantly being redrafted and promulgated. The principles behind the efforts of business associations have been set forth in *The Royal Bank of Canada Monthly Letter:* "(1) That I ought to promote my own greater good rather than my own lesser good; (2) that I ought to promote the greatest good on the whole; (3) that, in the distribution of good, I ought, so far as my action can secure it, to regard one man's good as being equally valuable with the like good of another. These have been called the axioms of Prudence, Rational Benevolence, and Equity."(6)

The public's judgment of the ethics and morality of U.S. business does not support the jaundiced views of social critics that regularly reach the headlines. Managers who head U.S. businesses are respected by the public at large, and their ethical standards are judged favorably in comparison with those of their counterparts in public office and in labor unions. However, corporate executives rank relatively far down the list of leader groups in the minds of the general public. Public confidence ranged in the following order from highest esteem to least esteem, according to a public opinion poll (7) conducted by the Opinion Research Corporation: scientists, physicians, college professors, lawyers, federal officials, *small businessmen,* public relations executives, average workers, local officials, *corporate executives,* advertising executives, labor union leaders.

Not surprisingly, the corporate executives who were polled think they deserve a higher rating than the general public gives them; they place themselves, not at the top, but in fourth place after scientists, college professors, and physicians. Corporate executives agree with the public rating of labor union leaders at the bottom of the list from the standpoint of their adherence to ethical and moral practices.

This opinion poll found that in the public's conception morality and social responsibility were almost undistinguishable and that, among other things, an ethical company will

- Design products to serve customers better.
- Supply useful information on what products will do and how best to use them.
- Attempt to raise popular tastes rather than cater to the mediocre.
- Act as a responsible community citizen.
- Protect employees' jobs, within its capability, against the hazards attendant upon abrupt technological change.

Executive Behavior

> In my opinion man is dominated neither by the will-to-pleasure (Freud) nor by the will-to-power (Adler), but by what I call the will-to-meaning; that is to say, his deep-seated striving and struggle for a higher and ultimate meaning to his existence. This is his mission in life —his unique task.
>
> —VICTOR FRANKEL

Executives are people, and they behave like people. They are tempted by small and petty diversions from the right path, and they have individual personal bents and blind spots of their own. Henry Ford's introducing leadership in innovations into the auto industry and his resounding success in the process did not prevent him in his later years from developing rigid and unrealistic thinking on such matters as the ill-fated Peace Ship and his support of the anti-Semitic campaigns of a local newspaper. But in general the successful manager, after he has reached a certain level of achievement in terms of material wealth, power, and prestige, tends to nurture the issues and values toward which he feels strongly empathetic. If he is a normal human being, those values and issues concern the welfare of the society of which he is a part.

In times past, the Machiavellian manners and values of some businessmen received much publicity and overshadowed the good works of the more socially responsible leaders. Society has regulated the present business scene to such an extent that a head-high, forthright ethical posture for the manager is necessary for both prestige and survival. Society will no longer tolerate ruthlessness on the part of the manager; he can no longer behave unethically when he gets down to business matters.

AMA's Lawrence A. Appley has been one of the most articulate spokesmen for the social responsibility of the businessman. In a talk presented at a leadership conference (8), he summed up this social responsibility in these words:

> A thoughtful leader is one who continually studies what he is doing in life and what he is getting out of life, and what others receive from life because of him. In business terms, this means that he provides time, effort, staff, and money to develop the finest products and services that can be distributed, to put into practice the finest code of ethics that it is possible for men to follow, to plan well the impact that his business is to have over a long period of time, to organize all resources into fine, dynamic outfits, and to furnish the kind of leadership which inspires confidence, respect, and pride. It is a man's responsibility to society to waste neither himself nor others. He must devote his life to getting the most out of both.

References

[1] Edward C. Bursk, Donald T. Clark, and Ralph W. Hidy, eds., *World of Business* (New York: Simon & Schuster, Inc., 1962), Vol. 1, pp. 9–10.

[2] Herbert J. Muller, "The Quarrel That Shouldn't Be," *The Presidents Forum* (Spring/Summer 1965), pp. 5–9.

[3] "Company Social Responsibility—Too Much or Not Enough?" *The Conference Board Record* (April 1964).

[4] Grace J. Finley, "Business Defines Its Social Responsibilities," *The Conference Board Record* (Nov. 1967).

[5] "Why Are We in Business?" *Management Record* (Dec. 1961), pp. 2–7.

[6] "Self-Regulation in Business," *The Royal Bank of Canada Monthly Letter* (Sept. 1964).

[7] "The Ethics of American Business." Research Report of *The Public Opinion Index for Industry* (Princeton: Opinion Research Corp., Aug. 1964).

[8] Lawrence A. Appley, "Responsibilities of Business Leadership." Address before General Electric Leadership Conference, Association Island, New York (1954).

Additional Readings

Peter F. Drucker, "Big Business and the National Purpose," *Harvard Business Review* (March–April 1962).

John W. Gardner, *Self-Renewal: The Individual and the Innovative Society* (New York: Harper & Row, Publishers, Inc. 1964).

PART THREE:
Power

Human beings are complex organisms, and it is never an easy thing to analyse the motives involved in their behavior. The fact is that the individual himself is rarely able to give a satisfactory account of the motives for his conduct, since the elements entering into it are both numerous and complex. One should therefore be wary in attempting to interpret the behavior of others.

—M. F. ASHLEY MONTAGU

IX. Behavioral Basics

OF all the modern axioms proposed to permit greater insight into management's future course, perhaps the most controversial is the theory that managers must accept and study the basic behavioral characteristics of man. "Practical" managers will ignore the misty area of human behavior and confine their ideas of good management to using what you have, or what you can get, to get what you're after.

Such a dated concept of good management has its roots in the turbulent early days of human organization, when "management" philosophy and organizational decorum were based on the historical experiences and concepts of the internal organization of the early church, the early military regimes, and the earlier forms of state and national government, which developed various codes and laws concerned with human behavior.

It has been only in the twentieth century that codes of conduct, philosophies of organization, and more definitive concepts of human behavior have been brought to focus on the management discipline as we consider it today.

The management function is concerned primarily with the members of the organization being managed and the forces of society in the form of government, consumer, supplier, investor, and the other publics that impinge upon the modern enterprise. As aptly stated by Lyndall F. Urwick, "Medicine is the only other art besides management that deals all the time with human beings."

Thus the basic needs and motivation of people are keystones in the organizational relationships of modern management. To list these behavioral aspirations, attitudes, motivations, and the like would be to attempt to cover the broad and expanding subject matter of sociological, anthropological, and psychological research and the newer composite studies of the behavioral scientist. The purpose of this chapter is not to attempt to collate the entire field of knowledge on this topic but to point up the importance of basic behavioral characteristics in both the individual and the organizational group in the management scheme.

The essentially political nature of current-day corporations, stressing the role of formal personnel administration in managerial success, is now well recognized by most managers. Studies of the formal and informal organizations that exist and persist in companies is a fascinating aspect of modern business. Both formal and informal organizations manifest certain basic behavioral characteristics, and behavioral scientists studying them have a tendency to specialize in fragmented areas of basic behavior. This fragmentation caused UCLA Professor Harold Koontz to use the phrase "the management-theory jungle" to describe the current state of management theory.

Earlier in this century, management thought was dominated by practicing executives and engineers, and out of this domination came the now classic body of so-called scientific management. This was embellished and augmented with certain doctrines recognizing the personnel factor, and more recently the social scientist's influence has been taking command of management theory in the Free World and is replacing the former authoritarian doctrines with values that are more democratic and more human.

Business Week (1) puts it this way: "The executive at the center of all this theorizing can catalogue the academic wildlife around him in much simpler fashion: On his left, the more radical behaviorists and social system theorizers; to his right, the more conservative decision theorists and mathematical model makers; and perhaps closer to his own position, some of the human relationists and the empiricists."

Perhaps the word for the study of behavioral basics in management should be *praxiology,* which Webster defines as "a proposed science of conduct and its disorders." The professional praxiologist or people-centered manager is by nature a student of the underlying principles of behavior that exist in the men and women coming within his management purview. Managers, whose job by definition is to deal all the time with human beings, must study the basic behavioral characteristics that are vital to understanding manpower resources and the proper functioning of these resources in management.

Behavioral Science: What It Is

Louis E. Newman, president of Smithcraft Corporation, tells how he once asked, "What do you mean by a behavioral scientist?" and got the answer, "That is what someone is called when he gets a grant from the Ford Foundation." (2) The term was indeed coined by the Ford Foundation, and it appears to be a more acceptable term now than "social science" or "sociology," which has political overtones. Behavioral science is a storehouse of important systematic information on man's behavior, based on the approach and point of view of the scientist.

This storehouse of important statements, which seem to stand up under scientific scrutiny, covers a vast range of subjects. A recent compilation lists 1,045 generalizations that are drawn from the fields of psychology, sociology, and anthropology. Mainly oriented from data on modern Western man, these statements range widely. In this compilation, *Human Behavior—An Inventory of Scientific Findings,* Bernard Berelson and Gary A. Steiner have pointed out that "human behavior is far more variable, and therefore less predictable, than that of any other species." (3)

The empirical image that emerges here is somewhat disturbing. Those who place "reason" in the forefront of human behavior will not find confirmation and support in the study. Those who believe in biological inheritance as a major determiner of human behavior will find that "behavioral-science man is social man—social product and social seeker." Those who believe in self-interest as the primary motive behind human behavior will discover that, as John F. Kennedy has written, man is a "creature making others and made by others."

Studies of Behavior

Organizational behavior has been studied in recent years with various degrees of sophistication in the military, government, academic, church, and business fields. New groups have sprung from the fields of sociology, psychology, psychiatry, anthropology, political science, management science, administrative science, and economics to pursue organizational behavior from various basic approaches. Cross-disciplinary studies and interdisciplinary research interlace the area of the behavioral scientist so that it is difficult to avoid overlap.

In all this, there is increasing emphasis by behavioral scientists on study of the organization itself, rather than study of broad institutional problems or problems of the individual. The major variables of task, structure, technology, and people are central for any behavioral-science approach to organization, and the modern approach calls for research in better methods of analysis and implementation. (4)

Stuart Chase, in *The Proper Study of Mankind* (5), has pointed out:

The laws of culture are something like Boyle's Law of Gases. An individual person, like a molecule of hydrogen, is unpredictable. But there is a definite pattern which the whole group will follow, and which can be statistically described. We know, for instance, how many will be born, how many will marry, how many classrooms will be needed in the years ahead. If an observer charts the pattern, he can predict behavior with reasonable probability.

Sherlock Holmes, philosophizing on Boyle's Law of Gases, said to his friend Watson: "While the individual man is an insoluble puzzle, in the aggregate he becomes a mathematical certainty. You can never foretell what any one man will do, but you can say with precision what an average number will be up to. Individuals vary but percentages remain constant."

Rensis Likert, director of the Institute for Social Research and professor of psychology and sociology at the University of Michigan, has led an intensive $4 million research program since 1947 to determine the forms of organizational structures, management principles, and practices used by managers who are achieving the best results in American business and government. This study undergirds his excellent *New Patterns of Management* (6), which is addressed to all persons concerned with the problems of organizing human resources and activity, especially managers.

Several important forces and resources, Likert indicates, are causing an acceleration of management interest in behavioral science. The forces include the changes taking place in American society that give the individual greater freedom and initiative plus the resulting changes in attitude, the greater educational level of the labor force, U.S. cultural trends, the increasing concern about mental health, the increasing complexity of technology, and the growing dissatisfaction of management people with the theories and practices inherited from the past.

Technical Change and Organizational Behavior

Dale Carnegie's *How to Win Friends and Influence People,* published in 1936, was a precursor of publicly available psychological studies in the realm of overcoming resistance to change. More recent research has tended to indicate that Carnegie's model was not so technically foolish as was thought upon its first appearance, when it was tagged as a slick system of dubious integrity.

Even earlier, the Hawthorne researches of the late 1920s sought for change through catharsis rather than change by the Dale Carnegie type of face-to-face influence through a warm personal relationship developed and used for bargaining purposes. During the 1920s and 1930s, the major problem was the impact of technical change on the organizations that were forming and expanding in that growth period. The effect of change on an organization was barely understood in those simpler management days, and it was certainly not high on the manager's priority list of problems. In more recent years, research has shed light on the organizational aspects of change, particularly as it concerns innovation from a technical viewpoint, significant changes in jobs, the effect of automated processes, and the influence of more sophisticated instrumentation and systems concepts. These phenomena offer a fertile field for modern anthropologists, and more and more of these specialists are finding prominent places in government and foundation efforts in the newer, less industrialized countries around the world.

The effect of change is well expressed in Charles H. Savage, Jr.'s recent Cornell-Harvard study (7), which is summarized in the following statement:

Technical change is socially disruptive. This is the nature of the beast. As each new technique is spanked into life, the older order dies a little—an outcome ordained by the condition of inter-relatedness that exists between the technical and social dimensions of reality.

In a developing economy, it is the technologist who presides—untutored and usually unwittingly—over this process. Around his person swirls the backwash of malaise which is always the lot of the innovator—a circumstance that he endures with only the most rudimentary understanding of the forces that he has unsettled and the playback that he is experiencing.

In the struggle for survival and growth, managers must continually break through new levels of performance, and there is a recognizable sequence of events by which a manager accomplishes this breakthrough. The maintenance of the newly attained level of performance requires recognition of another sequence of events. The breakthrough sequence involves technical and social change and must deal with the accompanying resistance to change and the existing cultural pattern.

The behavior of people affected by a technical change, with its accompanying social effect, is very complex. As J. M. Juran (8) says:

It stems from the myriads of habits and beliefs which the human being derives from the numerous groups and circles, i.e., societies, of which he is a part. To understand all this requires a journey into the nature of human motivation. This brings us to the work of the behavioral scientists, since the real experts in human motivation are these scientists, *not* the managers. Unfortunately the behavioral scientists have not translated their findings fully into the manager's dialect. We must, therefore, get just a bit acquainted with the dialect of these scientists.

Evolution of Behavioral Science in Management

Yesterday's managers often have a romantic aura about them that is hard to match in the current business period, despite noble efforts by some business periodicals to dramatize the triumphs and tribulations of executives on the world management stage. Henry Ford, Cornelius Vanderbilt, Harvey Firestone, Andrew Carnegie, and many others stirred and inspired their organizations toward goals that were as clear as crystal to the organizations involved. The administrative techniques of managing these organizations were in many cases instinctive, improvised, varied, and generally more primitive than the methods used today. They were also colorful, haphazard, and individualized, but in general they overlooked the needs of the people in the organizations.

As enterprises grew larger, particularly in the United States, the need for better management became apparent. Systematic study of the problems encountered then led to fractionation of the larger management area into smaller parts for the purpose of study.

Some of the management pioneers in American industry during the early 1900s dipped into the structural and operational aspects of human organization sufficiently to lay a foundation of principles that are today being polished up and promoted under the banner of behavioral science. This relatively new grouping of studies in psychology, anthropology, and sociology is becoming essential to the modern manager's philosophy, skills, patterns of thought, and actions.

Robert C. Sampson, in his book on *Managing the Managers* (9), makes a basic distinction between two separate systems of management: the efficiency-oriented management engineering system and the management-behavioral system. The latter, to use Norbert Wiener's terminology, is primarily concerned with the human use of human beings.

The earlier management pioneers were heavily oriented toward the scientific management and engineering approach, with emphasis on its measurement aspects. Through the years, that field has been well plowed, and the newer contributors are working the behavioral fields for guidance in management affairs. The pragmatic approach of industrial psychology arises from the fact that it is dealing with large numbers of people and this sponsors statistical rather than individual analyses. From the empirical findings of the traditional studies much has been learned about many aspects of the man at work, but until rather recently the systematic study of his personality has been neglected.

The Taylor period. At a time when Henry Ford's Model T was celebrating its first birthday, Frederick Winslow Taylor, a Philadelphia engineer, was introducing a new way of thinking about management as a planning, organizing, and controlling force based on methods Taylor had been developing for 30 years in the steel industry. The new philosophy of scientific management was proposed as a solution to the wasteful operations of the Eastern railroads through the installation of an incentive wage system that penalized substandard performance.

Despite opposition from labor, Taylor's principles of scientific management laid a foundation stone in the introduction of the scientific attitude toward management, the recognition of a concept of cooperation, and the importance of developing each individual to his greatest efficiency and prosperity as a principal goal of good management.

The Hawthorne experiments. The Hawthorne experiments at Western Electric in the late 1920s tapped the growing trend evolving from World War I—a combination of the engineer's approach to management with the psychologist's emphasis on testing and welfare plans as a contribution. The Hawthorne team sought to study the behavior of the employees themselves in an effort to improve personnel administration from a standpoint other than "executive thought and action." Out of this came a bible of the human relations movement: *Management and the Worker,* by Professor Fritz Roethlisberger and W. J. Dickson (10), which proclaimed the importance of human relations in the equation of management.

Business Week (11) has pointed out the seminal character of the Hawthorne experiments:

> References to the famous experiments abound, but so many specialists have since developed their own particular approaches that human relations theory now forms one of the more tangled thickets within the management-theory jungle. Today the industrial woods are full of behavioral-science consultants, mental hygienists, sensitivity trainers, personnel counselors, communications experts, group dynamicists, attitude testers, nondirective interviewers, program analysts, role-playing instructors, and executive developers—all taking off from the classic concepts of Hawthorne.

The efficiency period. In the same period as the Hawthorne study, there emerged a trend of devotion to industrial efficiency. The prime mover in this trend was Harrington Emerson, the "high priest of efficiency," who flourished in the United States after his early European experiences, his Alaskan university tenure, and his consulting career. Emerson, who was credited with introducing standard costs, tabulating machines for accounting, and line and staff organization into industrial management, codified his ideas on waste elimination in one of the earliest guides to better management and advocated the approach of good staff guidance in the managerial areas as distinct from the technical problems of manufacture.

Emerson's work was an important thrust in the recognition of the behavior of managers and their associates as a distinct area for study, which was different from the area in vogue among the industrial engineers of the day.

Mooney's organizational concepts. James David Mooney, former president of General Motors Export Corporation, was responsible for a far-flung international industrial empire in the era that followed World War I and extended into World War II, during which time he pioneered in management thought from the base of his prodigious historical research. He conceived the idea that principles of organization were the same for all organizations throughout history: Religious, government, military, educational, and industrial groups all followed his "scalar principle," which embodied the hierarchical structure that he described as prevailing in them.

Although Mooney's publications are seldom featured in the behavioral studies of today, they did put into perspective the concepts and relationships of an organization operating in any sphere of endeavor in which management becomes a challenge.

Harry Hopf. Harry Arthur Hopf, a London-born, German-educated immigrant, was active in this same period of management thought. By 1938 he had produced a large number of writings and speeches on management philosophy and practice, particularly the scientific approach to the solution of office and administrative problems in the banking and insurance industries. Harrington Emerson's zeal for efficiency had inspired Hopf's first investigations, which led him to become one of America's foremost management spokesmen. Consultant to the government and many large firms, he was an expert on problems of organization and administrative control, further establishing this area of managerial endeavor as a behavioral environment for special recognition.

The Clark contribution. Wallace Clark, a quiet American management consultant who died in 1948, left a wealth of material on management know-how and the ideal managerial characteristics of efficiency, democracy, profitability, and humaneness. His consulting activity throughout the world became so persuasive that his name became a verb, as managers learned to "clark" a plant to increase its productivity, improve working conditions, and break down social barriers to opportunity. Clark's original approach to managerial problems was a liberal-arts-oriented attack, which, abetted by the scientific philosophy of the times, mellowed his contribution with an emphasis on the mental as well as the physical hindrances to the free flow of work. Clark's insight was another building block in the management philosophy that separates the task of managing people from that of managing machines. (12)

Gantt charts. In the early twentieth century, Henry Laurence Gantt devised his Gantt charts for keeping track of idle time, the output of individuals, work planning, and factory control. More and more, he was convinced that employee morale and motivation also were vital to managerial success, and his writings did a great deal to foster training within industry. A successful management consultant, he contributed greatly to the recognition of the worker's behavior, like that of his manager, as the key to success in industry.

Dennison's innovations. One-time president of the Dennison Manufacturing Company, Henry S. Dennison won worldwide management recognition in the 1930s and 1940s with his psychological insights into the management problems of that day and the need to supplement scientific management with all the available knowledge of the social sciences. Dennison used his factories as a laboratory in which to experiment in all things new in the management area: among them employee testing, committee organization, methods analysis, and a unique scheme that provided nontransferable common stock for employees, thus making them controlling partners and profit sharers in the corporation. An unusual sense of public responsibility encouraged Dennison to recognize the social and behavioral side of the business equation at a time when the emphasis was still on the production and engineering aspects of industry.

Management as a profession. Until his death in 1955, Harlow Stafford Person, educated formally as an economist, was a major contributor to the concept of a profession of management. Years earlier, he had advocated joining the work of the industrial engineer with that of the social scientist in assessing the social values of any industrial proposal. As a contributor, in 1935, to *The Encyclopedia of Social Sciences,* he broadened the scope of the scientific-management movement beyond Taylor's narrower concepts to embrace the contribution of the social scientist. Later on, he refined this to include the behavioral scientist.

Recent Research in Behavioral Science

In the past 20 years, an enormous amount of research has been done on the problems of people at work. Methodology, techniques, and points of view vary widely; innumerable elements of the management scheme are being probed by students in the field.

The work of Rensis Likert, at the Institute for Social Research, on the role of the individual as a member of a group; the work of Chris Argyris of Yale on the need of a person to retain his individuality in an organization; the Theory X and Theory Y concept of Douglas McGregor, stressing respect for workers as persons and allowing freedom in the job; the theories of the work-centered psychologists, such as Frederick Herzberg; the practitioner approach of Robert C. Sampson; the work of the economists, anthropologists, psychiatrists, and industrial sociologists—all are well presented in many current books available to managers.

These many contributions are gradually being integrated into the basic knowledge of the behavioral sciences, which can be of increasing usefulness to thoughtful managers. (13, 14)

Behavioral Basics in Action

"The ability to control the behavior of its members," Victor H. Vroom (15) has stated, "is a prerequisite of a viable organization."

For more than 20 years, Britain's Glacier Metals Co. Ltd., which produces machine and motor bearings at a level of about $50 million per year, has subjected itself to an objective analysis of its own workings. (16) This study, the result of a collaboration between the chairman and a psychoanalyst, has dealt with the psychological and sociological gears and balance wheels of the business enterprise. It was started as a government-sponsored project in 1948.

One of the interesting findings has to do with the three systems that can be distinguished as operating simultaneously within the company: the executive system, the representative system, and the legislative system, which interact with each other and with other factors in the management activity. Other findings concern the area of wages and salaries, the "time span of discretion," the individual's growth, and career patterns.

Some 30 British companies are experimenting with the application of Glacier Project ideas, several Netherlands companies are investigating what may be of value to them, and the principles are being introduced in case form at the Harvard Business School.

The Study of Behavior

The Harvard Business School's case method of study has long stressed the behavioral aspects of business situations. In the schedule for a recent year, 22 out of a total of 207 programmed hours in the Advanced Management Program are devoted to "Human Behavior in Organizations," in addition to 10 hours in business simulation and

21 hours in case studies where the behavioral aspects of factual management situations also are considered.

One of the best laboratories for learning about behavior is, obviously, actual management practice, where the ability to deal with human behavior is developed in actual situations. As George Copeman states, "Many people have become successful business managers without studying management. This is a credit to their intelligence and personality (including their inner drive), and hence to their ability to feel for and understand the kind of behavior which makes for a good executive."(17)

Copeman presents his laws of business management, which deal with such areas as economic authority, planning, control, and organization structures, with the suggestion that a test of a law's general validity should be an examination of "the general behavior of business organizations or their executives, divorced from any wishful thinking about how organizations and executives should behave or how it is imagined they behave."

Successful management, while a credit to the executive's knowledge of such tools of management as accounting, market research, and planning, also involves an understanding of the laws and behavioral code of management, which can be gained by experience and improved with study.

The problem of studying behavior in business organizations is complex, owing to the large number of variables. With improved systems and computer concepts, however, great strides have been made in the area of simulation. For example, the U.S. Office of Naval Research, through the Carnegie Institute of Technology and the Western Management Science Institute (18), has been using simulalation as a tool of research to reproduce and study business systems. This work has been extended into organizational theory research—a study of the total management system—with constructs drawn from economics, accounting, and psychology. Thanks to computer simulation, the effects of plans, controls, and the personality factors ascribed to the various managers in a hypothetical firm can be studied in terms of their effect on the operations of the company.

One result of the study is the development of an "index of felt pressure," which is determined for each individual in the firm and illustrates the sum total of the various pressures exerted on him. The formal pressures affecting, for example, a particular salesman—plus such informal factors as personality conflicts with his superior—can be put into this model. Some salesmen meet increased pressure by increasing effort and selling more; others react adversely, so that sales decline. As pressure diminishes, on the other hand, the phenomenon called "organizational slack" develops, and the firm's efficiency suffers.

To get back to more specific instances of behavioral basics in action: E. F. Scoutten, vice-president of The Maytag Company, writes in NICB's *Business Management Record* (19) about an interesting case at his own company a few years ago:

> At The Maytag Company we have had a standard-hour, methods-time measurement job incentive system. For years we thought it was just common sense that the employee was favorably inclined toward the foreman who was lenient and let him, on occasion, shortcut the method or otherwise deviate in an effort to increase his earnings. A number of years ago, however, we had Bob Kahn's [Robert L. Kahn, Professor of Psychology, Uni-

versity of Michigan] group from the University of Michigan do a very thorough, and awfully expensive, survey of our employees' attitudes. It was worth every cent we put in it, because among other things we made the amazing discovery, which didn't square with common sense, that the vast majority of the employees much preferred a foreman who was strict and who insisted that they follow the methods set forth in the labor standard minutely. It took us a lot of time to convince our foremen that this was the kind of foreman the workers wanted; but I have no doubt about the validity of the study.

In *My Years with General Motors* (20), Alfred P. Sloan, Jr. points out how the behavioral aspects of one crisis affected the organizational structure of the corporation.

A conflict arose in 1921–1922 between the research organization and the producing divisions, along with a parallel conflict between the top management of the corporation and divisional management. The bone of contention was a revolutionary car with an air-cooled engine of "Boss" Kettering's design that used copper fins to dissipate engine heat. The executive committee imposed this radical car design on the Chevrolet and Oakland Divisions on the basis of preliminary research indications that the new engine would prove successful. When the car failed in its first tests and experienced difficulty a year later on its second testing, corporate policy had to be shifted to establish a dual program of water-cooled and copper-cooled engines. During still another year of continuing development and testing, considerable organizational tension arose among the research organization, the divisions, and top management over the ultimate success of the new engine. Finally, in May 1923, an impartial engineering evaluation resulted in placing the project on a longer-range basis.

(Many years later, the Corvair appeared with an air-cooled engine, using some of the principles of the original research work.)

Tension and strife during this period were so great that Kettering offered his resignation. The issue, basically, was, can fundamental work be continued and supported in the face of events outside the laboratory that adversely affect the development and are not pertinent to the fundamental principles involved? Kettering did not resign, but the episode had profound effects on the organizational relationships of the entire General Motors Corporation. In Mr. Sloan's words:

> The significant influence of the copper-cooled engine was in what it taught us about the value of organized cooperation and coordination in engineering and other matters. It showed the need to make an effective distinction between divisional and corporate functions in engineering, and also between advanced product engineering and long-range research. The copper-cooled engine episode proved emphatically that management needed to subscribe to, and live with, just the kind of firm policies of organization and business that we had been working on. Altogether, the experience was to have important consequences in the future organization of the corporation.

Perhaps a parallel study of the behavioral implications of this work would have saved General Motors time and development money. Lyndall F. Urwick (21), internationally renowned authority on management, states the perspective of behavioral science succinctly in an article in *Personnel* magazine:

> Henry le Châtelier, the physicist who introduced the work of Frederick Taylor to France, once said that scien-

tific method consists of six steps—definition, analysis, measurement, hypothesis, experiment, and proof, *in that order*. As far as I can see, the claims of some representatives of the behavioral sciences to a lion's share of the contributions to our knowledge of managing and their anxiety to embark on step three—measurement—have served only to confuse the progress made in the first four decades of this century in the first two steps—definition and analysis. In particular, they have made the terminology of the subject extremely disorderly.

Aside from being unnecessary, this is an embarrassment to practicing managers, who have to use such knowledge as we possess here and now. In fact, it merely endorses Mayo's castigation of such sciences as "unsuccessful" on the grounds of their failure to convey skills that are "directly usable in human situations"!

References

[1] "Management Pattern—Some Trophies from the 'Jungle,'" *Business Week* (Feb. 16, 1963), p. 140.

[2] "Behavioral Science—What's in It for Management," *Business Management Record* (June 1963), pp. 32–44. National Industrial Conference Board Management Conference, New York (Jan. 1963).

[3] Bernard Berelson and Gary A. Steiner, *Human Behavior—An Inventory of Scientific Findings* (New York: Harcourt, Brace & World, Inc., 1964).

[4] William W. Cooper, Harold J. Leavitt, and Maynard W. Shelly II, *New Perspectives in Organization Research* (New York: John Wiley & Sons, Inc., 1964), Chapter 4.

[5] Stuart Chase, *The Proper Study of Mankind* (New York: Harper & Bros., 1956), pp. 72, 136.

[6] Rensis Likert, *New Patterns of Management* (New York: McGraw-Hill Book Co., 1961).

[7] Charles H. Savage, Jr., Monograph No. 7 of the Society for Applied Anthropology (Ithaca: Cornell University, 1964).

[8] J. M. Juran, *Managerial Breakthrough* (New York: McGraw-Hill Book Co., 1964).

[9] Robert C. Sampson, *Managing the Managers: A Realistic Approach to Applying the Behavioral Sciences* (New York: McGraw-Hill Book Co., 1965).

[10] F. J. Roethlisberger and W. J. Dickson, *Management and the Worker* (Cambridge: Harvard University Press, 1939).

[11] "Workers Can Be a Team, Too," Management Famous Firsts, *Business Week* (April 1964).

[12] "Carrying the Gospel to Europe," Milestones of Management, *Business Week* (April 1964).

[13] Douglas McGregor, *The Human Side of Enterprise* (New York: McGraw-Hill Book Co., 1960).

[14] Douglas McGregor, *The Professional Manager* (New York: McGraw-Hill Book Co., 1967).

[15] Victor H. Vroom, "Some Psychological Aspects of Organizational Control," *Seminar on the Social Science of Organizations,* sponsored by the Ford Foundation at the University of Pittsburgh (June 10–23, 1962).

[16] Management: "Playing Guinea Pig," *Business Week* (Nov. 7, 1964), pp. 166–170.

[17] George Copeman, *Laws of Business Management* (London: Business Publications Ltd., 1962), Chapter 11.

[18] Charles P. Bonini, "Simulating Organizational Behavior," in *New Perspectives in Organization Research* (New York: John Wiley & Sons, Inc., 1964).

[19] The Conference Board, *Business Management Record* (June 1963), p. 39.

[20] Alfred P. Sloan, Jr., *My Years with General Motors* (New York: Macfadden Bartell Books, 1965), p. 94.

[21] Lyndall F. Urwick, "Have We Lost Our Way in the Jungle of Management Theory?" *Personnel* (May–June 1965), pp. 8–18.

Additional Readings

M. F. Ashley Montagu, *Man's Most Dangerous Myth: The Fallacy of Race,* fourth revised edition (Cleveland: World Publishing Co., 1964).

C. Northcote Parkinson, *The Evolution of Political Thought* (Boston: Houghton Mifflin Co., 1958).

Mason Haire, *Psychology in Management* (New York: McGraw-Hill Book Co., 1956).

The key to social dynamics that Marx found in wealth and Freud in sex Bertrand Russell finds convincingly in Power.

—Harold Nicolson in *The Daily Telegraph*

x. The Powers That Be

Among the prominent issues focused in the public mind today are the powers that corporations and labor unions possess, the accountability of the power wielders, and the role of large unions and large corporations in the total power structure of the nation.

The Nature and Forms of Power

Power in the management structure needs to be recognized and understood as a vital force affecting all managers of tomorrow's enterprises. In a brilliant study first appearing in 1938, Bertrand Russell attempted to prove that the fundamental concept in social science is power, in the same sense in which energy is the fundamental concept in physics. He set forth the chief infinite desires of man as those for power and glory. "As a rule, however, the easiest way to obtain glory is to obtain power; this is especially the case as regards the men who are active in relation to public events. The desire for glory, there-

161

fore, prompts in the main the same actions as are prompted by the desire for power, and the two motives may, for practical purposes, be regarded as one." (1)

Russell makes a distinction among various forms of power over human beings: naked power, such as military and police power; power of propaganda; power of education; priestly or kingly power; revolutionary and economic power.

Power over human beings has always been a recognized measure of success, particularly in the leadership of men's minds. Whether the attainment of such power precedes a sense of compassion and social responsibility toward human beings or whether the reverse is true does not seem to matter much in the business world. The power seeker today has to be built that way inside, and it is doubtful that he has the lofty motives he may display when he has attained power. A successful manager, by the nature of his assignment as a manager, has access to considerable power over human beings in an economic sense, in an educational sense, in a propaganda sense, and most of all in an inspirational sense. For a manager to acknowledge these powers and use them in a balanced fashion for the general welfare of society is a true test of greatness.

The Power of Managers

James Burnham (2), writing at the beginning of World War II, predicted that professional managers were destined to become the primary holders of power in the United States' economic affairs and in society generally. His theory of managerial revolution is founded on a theory of the power struggle. He outlines the drive for power and privilege taking place in nations at different states of development and predicts:

> The managers will exercise their control over the instruments of production and gain preference in the distribution of products, not directly through property rights vested in them as individuals, but indirectly through their control of the state which in turn will own and control the instruments of production. The state—that is, the institutions which comprise the state—will, if we wish to put it that way, be the "property" of the managers. And that will be quite enough to place them in the position of ruling class.

Unless we learn to understand the fundamental nature and the interactions of the power systems in the scientific, business, political, and moral spheres, we will be, in the words of the late Professor Benjamin M. Selekman of Harvard, "in danger of failing in our mission, the mission to establish a great civilization on this continent and to lead the way toward peace and security for mankind." (3)

The managerial revolution of the past half-century, with its evolution of increasing managerial powers, has created a formidable power structure in the modern organization. Various degrees of authority, responsibility, and accountability are spelled out in the larger corporations by extensive manuals of procedure and control. The anatomy of the power of decision making is well recognized in a formal way in most large companies—certainly in such examples as General Motors, Du Pont, Standard Oil of New Jersey, U. S. Steel, Sears, Roebuck, First Na-

tional City Bank, Monsanto, and the New York Central
Railroad, to name just a few.

The individual power seekers, as well as those special
groups that seek to operate in the complex organizational
network of a large company today, present another aspect
of the power problem to the management of the corporation. The ambitions of the individual must be considered
along with the interests of the corporation itself, and this
often results in conflict. Most organized groups, such as
separate functional departments or labor unions, experience this conflict in the pursuit of their objective of attaining power for their particular group.

Such power drives, along with the reactions to them,
must be accommodated and directed by management at
each level to maintain organizational equilibrium with
adequate control over the profitable growth of the enterprise. The ranking leadership must have the profit motive
first in mind and still recognize the individual's desire for
power. Recognition must also be given to individuals of
talent who may never become administrative managers
but who contribute much and should have their power
urge fulfilled by recognition and honor.

The proposition that the measure of management is
the proper use of power, with the thesis that managers
should not restrict an individual's power but rather capitalize on its infinite potential, is the subject of *Managing
the Managers,* by Robert C. Sampson. (4) Here, the author
points out emphatically, "there is real danger that, without consideration of the behavioral sciences and with the
drive for engineering precision and for power in managing, decision making, planning, and improving will be
pulled into the hands of relatively fewer and fewer people.
Then there will be even more regimentation of manage-

ment people in jobs that are less and less challenging, interesting, and meaningful."

The power of managers is a matter for careful evaluation and understanding. It's there, it's used, and the successful manager must recognize it as a factor to be dealt with in organizational life.

Some Aspects of Power

Theories of power have always been fashionable in the political scene and in corporate life. From time to time, various establishments or interests (such as labor, Harvard economists, the Solid South, the steel industry, "Detroit," oil and gas, Wall Street, the munitions industry, the International Zionist conspiracy, the black power structure, and others) have been cited as power cliques that operate in our American society.

The very existence of the many power groups that flourish in our democratic free enterprise system emphasizes the fact that there can be no power elite in the United States. The coursing action of multiple power groups that clash, regroup, die, and are reborn in our society keeps it constantly agitated and sensitive to the evolving will of the people. "Power in America," sociologist David Reisman once wrote, "is situational and mercurial; it resists attempts to locate it."

A close examination of the various power groups in America will show that there are very few groups, or leaders of those groups, with a power span that covers the wide range of public concern. In the area of business and industry, there are few that cut across the wide spectrum of the industrial and business manager's purview. Power in the United States is marked more by compromise than by command and is characterized by ad hoc coalitions rather than stable alliances.

Machiavelli's realistic *Il Principe* (1532) lays down the sinister views of men in general that a prince must recognize if he is to attain and retain power. He sees the world of politics as a "jungle in which moral laws and standards of ethical conduct are merely snares for fools, a jungle in which there is no reality but power, and power is the reward of ruthlessness, ferocity, and cunning."

Such sinister premises of four centuries ago are now applicable to only a few selfish men of the type that will always exist in the economic environment of business. Business morality in the highly industrialized nations of the world has attained a vastly improved level, regardless of the fact that legislation, public opinion, and improved communications have aided in producing this better moral tone. Less developed business communities still foster certain power-minded individuals who undoubtedly obtain and maintain control by any means possible.

One theory of power that has been a subject of much discussion in the more mature societies and stabilized economies has to do with the power of vested interests. In corporate life the vested interests may be many, and labor disputes often provide examples of conflict between vested interests. As John Gardner puts it: "In any organization, many of the established ways of doing things are held in place not by logic or even by habit but by the force of one powerful consideration: Changing them would jeopardize the rights, privileges, or advantages of specific individuals—perhaps the president, perhaps the maintenance men." (5)

Power in the Organization

The activity and the peril that exist in a modern organization are concerned with both the individual career and the corporate life-and-death cycle. Because these two factors have such a different time span—the manager's career is finite, the corporation is theoretically immortal—there is a constant shifting of individual power within the organization. Externally, the corporation is always in a state of growth or decay, with a gradual increase or deterioration of power in the competitive and economic sense. The challenge of management is to control this shifting of power from without as well as from within.

Individual and small-group power. The power of individuals in small organizations is well recognized, perceptible, and accepted as the nature of the beast. The fact that the unit is small and power conflicts involve a relatively few people takes the problem out of public view. Even the tax collectors give comparatively little attention to the very small enterprise; the tax structure and our legal system tend to favor it.

The theory of games and the theory of strategy concern the elusive nature of the thread of opposition and conflict that runs through the various interrelationships of men, to use the words of John McDonald, *Fortune* editor. The power play between two or more individuals in a small organization can have as great an impact on the organization as the power drive of any large faction in a big corporation.

The small group possesses great power in the larger organization as well, if it has both a sense of purpose and a drive toward power. Management's knowledge of the character and temperament of small power groups within the company is vital to the health and proper growth of the enterprise. In an economic sense, however, the accretion of power by a large organization through growth from within or through the acquisition of strong small power groups is a matter of more concern to the business world.

Large-organization power. In the case of large, complex organizations, corporate power tends to have a straight-line relationship to corporate size. The tendency of large corporations to grow even larger—referred to by Anthony Sampson as "endemic elephantiasis"—is disturbing to many because of the power that these large organizations accumulate. Big Business, per se, is subject to attack by Big Government on the theory that bigness is unhealthy. Perhaps this government philosophy is a carryover from the old days of plundering when business was too often guilty of inadequate social consciousness and improper use of its concentrated power.

The ethical level of conduct encountered today in business is far above that of the past. As we have said, the prominent heads of large business corporations are today accepting their social responsibility to a pronounced degree.

Who Wields the Power?

The ultimate disagreements in business appear to be resolved through exercise of power by the chief executive. A recent study (6) of 50 vice-presidents in ten large U.S. companies, conducted by Ross Stanger, revealed that the most potent, and most often mentioned, influence toward accepting a "nonpreferred solution" was the chief executive's power. Regardless of the widespread decentralization and democratization of American industry, this study showed, the pattern is still authoritarian; resolution of conflict by appeal to higher authority is the rule.

But all power is not in the hands of top management. Lower echelons of the organization in many cases possess controlling power, at least to some extent, to say nothing of the obvious power of organized and recognized union groups. This power is implicit in control over personnel, information, instrumentalities, and resources, and it is both formal and informal. Thus, in spite of the chief executive's power, decision making is not all topside activity; it is shared to some extent by the switchboard operator, the receptionist, the executive secretary, the accountant, the public relations men, the personnel expert, and so on. Access to people and other information sources is a formidable means of power; knowledge is always potent.

The formal or informal control of power by various levels in large organizations is sometimes unrelated to delegated authority or assigned rank. A provocative case in a large mental hospital organization, cited by Thomas J. Scheff (7), illustrates the control that a subordinate group of hospital attendants had over the physicians through manipulation of the dependence of the physicians on the service group. The physicians' short tenure and disinterest in administration matters, plus the burden of administrative responsibility the physicians were expected to assume, led to an implicit trading agreement between attendants and physicians whereby the attendants took on certain obligations and responsibilities of the ward physicians in return for increased power to make decisions concerning patients. Failure of the individual physician to honor his part of the agreement resulted in complete lack of cooperation. He had difficulty in making a graceful entrance and departure from the ward, in keeping up with his paperwork, and in getting information. The attendants had the upper hand when any change was proposed, since they could refuse to assume responsibilities that were officially those of the ward physician but had previously been handled for him.

Similar informal power plays are found in the military, in educational and penal institutions, and in government bureaus, to say nothing of large corporations. Some factors that account for the power blocs in large organizations are increasing specialization (with the elite groups it creates), spatial relationships, the "grapevine," and coalitions that ignore normal organization structures. The answer for the manager is to identify and characterize the informal power structures that exist in his organization. Once he recognizes them, he can use them to advantage rather than have to react to them under unfavorable circumstances.

The formal power of a manager in the organization is based, of course, on his position, his rank, and the extent of authority and responsibility delegated to him. Various research findings tend to show that the formal, assigned status and the actual power of the supervisor, for example, will be closer together if four conditions prevail: First, the style of his supervision is compatible with the personality characteristics of his subordinates. Second, he reduces the degree of punitiveness inherent in his reactions to error. Third, the degree of pressure he exerts downward is considered reasonable. Fourth, the degree of autonomy available to him to plan his work and make decisions is substantial.

A theory pertinent to this power equilibrium has been

proposed by Douglas McGregor. His concept of participative management, Theory Y, designed to replace or at least soften authoritarian Theory X, envisages a shift from an all-powerful superior dealing with impotent subordinates to a more balanced power relationship that has been characterized as treating people as mature adults rather than as children. (8)

Ethics and Power

Ethel Watts Mumford, a not too recent American novelist, said that "knowledge is power, if you know it about the right person." In the early eighteenth century, Dr. Samuel Johnson perhaps anticipated Mrs. Mumford when he observed that nature has given women so much power that the law has very wisely given them little.

Women and men alike are driven by the fuel of their own philosophies, and we should be aware that sheer love of power drives some people. The tendency to strive for management power as an end in itself is a factor that cannot realistically be ignored when dealing with actual managers.

Career opportunity for the power-hungry manager becomes less and less certain as society enacts laws against unethical practices and public opinion in our culture fails to condone the swindler, the corporation pirate, the dictator, and the manipulator. The use of power is accepted in the ethics of our society under certain conditions and not accepted in other situations. So it is with the use or misuse of power in an organizational setup. The manager cannot have power as his primary objective in his corporate life and be as effective as the manager who uses his power ethically to further the goals of the individual and the organization, to free human capabilities rather than checkrein them.

Bertrand Russell selected four men who in his opinion possessed more power than any others—kings, emperors, presidents, military conquerors, or dictators. These were Buddha, Christ, Pythagoras, and Galileo. Their powers became effective through support of the state only after their philosophies and doctrines had achieved a great measure of success through propaganda. The common thread was the freeing of human life, rather than its enslavement, and this should be the guiding principle in the management of economic units. Control and domination by power are not ends in themselves. Rather, improvement in the well-being of those affected by the enterprise—employees, stockholders, customers, suppliers, and the public—should be the result.

Robert C. Sampson (4) put it well when he wrote:

Whatever the stage of history, whatever the particular marks of success, power is always there: owning men in slavery, controlling men in autocracy, saving their souls in religion. In the mastery of men, money, and materials, power has many forms—authority, prestige, influence, success, helping others, wealth, and service. Power is predominant in every facet of human behavior. The use, misuse, and abuse of personal and organizational power constitute the most perplexing problem in management. Although power wears many masks and is glossed over with many euphemisms, power per se is now the medium of management success. Too many managers pervert their authority to satisfy their personal power needs. The tragedy is that we have never learned because we have not been properly taught the dimensions of power and its proper use.

References

[1] Bertrand Russell, *Power: New Analysis* (New York: Barnes & Noble, 1962), pp. 8–9.

[2] James Burnham, *The Managerial Revolution: What Is Happening in the World* (New York: John Day Company, Inc., 1941), p. 72.

[3] Sylvia Kopald Selekman and Benjamin M. Selekman, *Power and Morality in a Business Society* (New York: McGraw-Hill Book Co., 1956), pp. 3–14.

[4] Robert C. Sampson, *Managing the Managers: A Realistic Approach to Applying the Behavioral Sciences* (New York: McGraw-Hill Book Co., 1965), p. 13.

[5] John W. Gardner, *Self-Renewal: The Individual and the Innovative Society* (New York: Harper & Row–Colophon Books, 1963), pp. 31–32.

[6] Ross Stanger, "Resolving Top-Level Managerial Disagreements," *Business Topics* (Winter 1965), pp. 15–22.

[7] Thomas J. Scheff, "Control over Policy by Attendants in a Mental Hospital," *Journal of Health and Human Behavior* (1961), pp. 93–105.

[8] Douglas McGregor, *The Human Side of Enterprise* (New York: McGraw-Hill Book Co., 1960).

Additional Readings

Mason Haire, *Organization Theory in Industrial Practice* (New York: John Wiley & Sons, Inc., 1962).

W. G. Bennis, K. D. Benne, and R. Chin, eds., *The Planning of Change: Readings in the Applied Behavioral Sciences* (New York: Holt, Rinehart & Winston, Inc., 1961).

xi. The Resonance Factor

FROM the electrical engineer's concept of resonance we
can draw a useful analogy of the value and importance of
resonance in management. A resonant management is a
group that automatically adjusts itself to maximize the
flow of communication, understanding, insight, concerted
action, and reaction when a socially oriented problem
arises or a management opportunity presents itself. A
resonant management will phase its action with the tide
of the problem or opportunity presented so that the structure and activity of the situation are brought in harmony
with the management structure and management activity,
thus increasing the stability of the enterprise and intensi-
fying the effect of its action.

Such sympathetic coordination of a group of top managers with each other and with the situation at hand is
difficult to formalize but readily recognizable when it oc-
curs. Like different instruments in an orchestra, the various executives are distinctive performers in their own
right, but all are in the same key, even though their contributions may be at different ends of the scale. In fact,

they may be in different octaves or registers but still resonant.

The promotable manager possesses certain personal and professional qualifications that are the subject of continual study by management savants. Significant advances have been made, particularly in the matter of selection and evaluation of managers. However, informal associations, unwritten laws, and bias exist in any human organization, and these affect the careers and promotability of executives. Important in this respect is the factor of the individual's personal resonance with his peers, his associates, and his subordinates.

Resonance is the ability of the manager to adjust personally to his leaders' or his associates' styles and moods harmoniously so the organization is stabilized and the common business effort is intensified, enriched, and supplemented by the informal rapport that results.

Discrimination in career advancement may result from misuse or abuse of resonance. The modern manager should recognize that there is such a factor in management and that it can be carefully and consciously used to his own advantage and that of the organization. Collegial resonance is a great thing in an organization if it is based on worthy rather than false criteria, intellectual rather than emotional rapport, organizational rather than purely personal concepts, and if it appreciates the values inherent in the conflict of ideas.

The shadows of nepotism, cronyism, seniority, social status, racism, eggheadedness, and Horatio Algeritis cast themselves in varying circumstances on the power groups that make up the resonant decision-making bodies of modern business enterprises. The effects vary considerably from the small management team to the larger sophisticated management committees and other organizational creatures that management employs, both formally and informally.

To understand the anatomy of the resonance phenomenon, to be able to assess its sympathetic vibrations, and to be able to adjust as appropriate is a challenge to the striving manager. Once the need for resonance of management thought and action is recognized, the entire management task can be intensified and enriched by supplementary "tuning in" on the part of subordinate management, to the end that the organizational resistance and friction that are so wasteful in the programs of a large enterprise are markedly reduced. A manager should thus be alert to the existence of resonance factors in both the upper and the subordinate sectors of the management hierarchy.

Requirements for Resonance

Propinquity is usually a prime requirement for a resonant management. Only by relaxed, face-to-face exposure and joint facing of problems can rapport be established on a lasting basis and qualify as true resonance. With improved communication facilities the need for intimate exposure is diminished, but long experience has shown that leadership influence varies directly with propinquity.

Napoleon's invasion of Russia in 1812 failed because of such organizational problems rather than because of the ravages of the popularly accused Russian winter. His 560,000-man army had to be reduced 40 percent so that guard units could be detached along the hard-pressed communication lines in the vast expanses of Russia as the troops approached Moscow. In this forbidding country these spread-out units foraged far and wide in the effort to find supplies to support themselves as they guarded the means of communication. With such disarray, they were easy prey for the Russians. Napoleon's personal drive and leadership could not span such vast distances and keep the polyglot soldier group in harmony with his objectives. There was no common cause strong enough to keep them from cracking under the strain. The severe winter did not become a factor until the retreat was already under way as a result of Napoleon's losing his grip on the morale and spirit of this scattered group.

The chief executive holds the key to creating a resonant top management team, for it is his philosophy, his inspiration, and his leadership that set a goal for all to strive toward. The success or failure of an enterprise depends, above all, on the relations of the top staff with the chief executive officer.

This is hardly news. Cardinal Richelieu expressed it (1) in his political testament:

> His Majesty the King having chosen His Consellors, it is for Him to put them in such a position that they can work for the grandeur and well-being of His Kingdom. Four principal things are required to this end.
> - The first, that His Majesty has confidence in them and they know he has;
> - The second, that he commands them to speak freely with him and assures them that they may do so without peril to them;
> - The third, that he treats them a bit liberally and that they believe that their services will not go uncompensated;
> - The fourth, that he empowers and maintains them so publically that they are assured that they have to fear

neither trickery nor the power of those who would wish their undoing.

The important responsibility for creating a resonant team places a primary people-picking task on the top executive—the task of selecting a harmonious yet often disparate collection of talented men who can counter as well as augment each other in group attacks on far-reaching long-term problems. If the chief executive cannot win the necessary allegiance and resonance from his top assistants, he must face up to replacing them with others with whom he may be able to create a sympathetic and stimulating interaction.

The ancient order of Saint Benedict recognized this need for mutual resonance in the monastery as a requirement for joining the order. This is attested by the rules laid down for the abbot by Saint Benedict:

> If any pilgrim monk come from distant parts, if with wish as a guest to dwell in the monastery, and will be content with the customs which he finds in the place, do not perchance by his lavishness disturb the monastery, but is simply content with what he finds, he shall be received for as long a time as he desires. If, indeed, he find fault with anything, or expose it, reasonably, and with the humility of charity, the Abbott shall discuss it prudently, lest perchance God has sent him for this very thing. But, if he have been found gossipy and contumacious in the time of his sojourn as guest, not only ought he not to be joined to the body of the monastery, but also it shall be said to him, honestly, that he must depart. If he does not go, let two stout monks, in the name of God, explain the matter to him.

In addition to sympathetic response from his top aides, the chief executive needs other resources. Sociologist W. I.

Thomas expressed these needs over a generation ago when he wrote of the four wishes of mankind. Every individual, he said, needed from his group four things: response, security, recognition, and new experience. (2)

Thus resonance—a sympathetic response from associates—is a universal desire of leaders and followers. The manager must recognize this factor in the complex management organizations of tomorrow and accept the proverb that "like begets like" as a useful, indeed necessary, parameter of the intimate top team that continually succeeds against the array of competition.

Resonance and the "Stud Factor"

The quality of management, in the final analysis, is dependent on the degree of resonance prevailing in the managerial hierarchy. This resonance is inversely proportional to the degree of friction that exists in the organization at the job interfaces between executives.

Management's overall achievement depends on its capacity to orchestrate this human activity in such a way as to integrate effort, reduce conflict, and minimize intraorganizational or functional friction. The sources of friction include poor-quality personnel, imperfect organizational structure, obstacles to communication, and faulty interpersonal relations. Though astute personnel administration, organizational planning, and advanced communication concepts are often employed, a degree of friction or dissonance may still persist if the management coalition is not a natural aggregation of personalities. Age, background, experience, education, ethics, intellectual prejudices, idiosyncrasies, and nepotism all may combine to produce patterns of resonance or dissonance that are not often recognized or analyzed in any way except by a general acknowledgment of those that are "in" and those that are "out" with the current administration. Such a tacit classification usually defies overt examination, and any dissonance is resolved only by intercorporate movement of executives, early retirement, static individual development, or career retrogression.

On the other hand, a group of managers with sympathetic working habits, mutual respect, and good social relations can symbiotically create a masterful combination for management. Such resonance can last throughout the careers of the individuals involved, but seldom is transferable in exactly the same form to successor management teams. The following generation of managers must somehow find the proper wavelength on which their conglomerate personalities can commune.

The process of achieving resonance and breeding it for later management cadres might be termed the *stud factor* in management. In its finest sense it is the breeding and upbringing of sequential and continuously evolving generations of resonant managers. As with the selective breeding processes used in the evolution of the Arabian horse and the collie dog, many generations of intelligent selection are required to create an outstanding "stable" of managerial talent.

In addition to careful selection, sufficient hybridization must occur to circumvent incestuous or anachronistic policies that persist long after they are ineffective. Although we live in a time of specialists, the chief executive officer must be an accomplished generalist. His general talents are necessary to provide well-rounded leadership and inspiration to those who would follow. These requirements are not unlike those for leadership in the clergy: A minister must be more than a specialist in preaching, teaching, fund raising, and counseling, to name just a few of the special skills in which he needs some proficiency. According to the *Christian Herald*, one study indicated that 93.8 percent of those men who become bishops are not especially good at any single pastoral skill but are passably capable in all of them.

The stud factor can further aid in creating an elite who win their management spurs by progressing through business obstacle courses and indoctrination in conventional and unconventional management techniques and strategies and who keeps their family relationships and obligations in proper perspective with the overwhelming demands of their executive careers.

There is the obvious hazard of a continuous stud line's deteriorating unless careful selection takes place. The chief executive must guard against such inbreeding in his management-replacement considerations. The words of George Bernard Shaw in *Man and Superman* are a good reminder: "The reasonable man adapts himself to the world. The unreasonable one persists in trying to adapt the world to himself. Therefore, all progress depends on the unreasonable man."

The stud factor in modern management has its roots in the systems of authority that historically prevailed within the business community and still exist today in some of the countries of the world. Sovereign rule by the head of the family and his successor is perhaps the most primitive system; it fits small enterprises almost anywhere, regardless of the country's state of industrialization. Many Middle Eastern, Far Eastern, and South American enterprises are ruled by this concept, and the family enterprise is very successful even in some highly developed economies, including those of the United States, the United Kingdom, and certain European countries.

The traditional German *Unternehmer* concept of those "born to lead" still persists in Europe to some degree, but it is waning under the impact of international competition. The patriarchal approach that characterizes French, Japanese, and Italian management thinking begets successive waves of managers by a stud system that is not necessarily nepotistic. At the other extreme in this spectrum of management authority systems is management by objectives, but even here the stud factor is important, and it must be recognized and employed intelligently to insure a resonant management core at all times.

Management by Crony

Slang and current terminology impute unsavory connotations to the word "crony," but these are not present in the word's Greek origin—*chronious,* meaning contemporary.

The derogatory undertones of "cronyism" perhaps stem from the emotional linkage that characterizes the intimate relationship that individuals may have with one another. An emotional attachment often hinders intellectual relationships; the intellectual's contemporaries are seldom if ever dubbed "cronies." Cronies are usually considered "favorites of the court," minions who respond to the bidding of the leader with little positive stand of their own.

However, cronies—in the original connotation of contemporaries—play an important part in the leadership function. The top man must have some trusted contemporaries who will act as a sounding board and, when necessary, offer loyal opposition to his proposals. Further, they must be men who will stick by the leader through thick and thin, no matter what the consequences. The good manager will select his contemporaries carefully to eliminate the sycophants, the hangers-on, and the weaklings. Just as the bridesmaids and groomsmen can enhance the main actors at the nuptials, so can the cabinet, the court, the adjutants, and the counselors enhance (or detract from) the manager's performance and accomplishments.

The Nepot

Of Harvard's class of 1965, 23 percent planned to do the same kind of work as their fathers. Just how many went into family businesses or professions, or landed successfully in large public corporations where their fathers were employed, is not known. The fact is that nepotism is far less widespread than is generally believed. Times are changing the demands on college graduates, and the new social class that is forming is based on intellect rather than family or social ties. Sociologist Digby Baltzell's WASPs—white Anglo-Saxon Protestants—have traditionally been the "in" group in U.S. business, but there is good evidence that the non-WASPs are no longer being flatly rejected. (3)

This is quite apparent from a recent study by Columbia University of the student bodies of select colleges. During the first half of this century, about two-thirds of the sons of prominent families in the New York *Social Register* went to Yale, Princeton, or Harvard—in that order. Now, less than 45 percent go to these three colleges; and the balance are dispersed, not among a dozen other colleges as formerly, but in about a hundred other schools.

Looking at business across the nation, rather than just at New York society, we find the Ivy League firmly entrenched. A statistical analysis released in May 1967 and based on 70,000 business leaders listed in Poor's *Register of Corporations, Directors, and Executives* indicated that the Ivy League schools' graduates are still capturing an increasing number of high corporate offices. Twenty years ago 41 percent of the collegians in the *Register* had an Ivy League diploma, whereas now this group is up to 47 percent. And, while the Ivies led the list, the number of college graduates versus noncollege graduates in the *Register* increased over the same period from 41.4 to 67.6 percent.

Selection procedures employed in business after the World War II student influx have tended to choose the academically gifted applicants rather than those with family or old school ties. As the ancient maxim goes, "pedigree won't sell a lame horse." The academic standing of the Ivy League schools, rather than the father-son factor, appears to be the attraction to business and industry.

Simultaneously, business and industry have been shifting away from family or social ties as a condition of executive employment, apparently on the theory that "he who boasts of his ancestors is like a potato—the best part of him is underground." The trend, in fact, is in the opposite direction, and in some cases there is undue discrimination against relatives of incumbent executives regardless of the talents of the candidate.

A *Harvard Business Review* study of nepotism confirmed the general feeling among 2,700 businessmen (some of whom were nepots) that nepotism is undesirable (60 percent), with 85 percent of the respondents considering nepots justifiable in specific situations where no nonrelatives are qualified and as many as 92 percent willing at least to go along with the idea of employing relatives in management. (4) This somewhat ambivalent response apparently results from the tendency of more executives to take a professional and objective approach to management, which enables them to justify nepotism in certain cases and reject it in others.

Relatives ordinarily fit in more easily than nonrelatives, and there are advantages to executives' having a similar background. For one thing, this reduces the need for re-examining basic philosophies and policies. Of course, it may work the other way and perpetuate an undesirable ingrown situation. Then, too, relatives may take a greater interest in the company, although this is a debatable point. Nepotism has a deterring effect on recruiting and at times spawns internal squabbling because of the possibility of favoritism, true or imagined.

Nevertheless, family businesses still play an important role in the American free enterprise system. Du Pont, Ford Motor, Reynolds Metals, Firestone, Weyerhaeuser, Standard Oil of New Jersey, Eli Lilly, Lincoln Electric, Dow Chemical, Seagrams, Corning Glass, Upjohn, and Cabot, Inc. are just a few of the U.S. firms that have a significant degree of family management and/or family proprietary interest. It has been estimated that 20 percent of *Fortune's* list of 500 largest manufacturing corporations show evidence of family management.

So far as resonance in management cadres is concerned, certainly nepots can reach unusual degrees of rapport (and, rarely, conflict). In any case, the aspiring manager must be prepared to cope with the nepotism that may occur in his organization.

Affinity Transcends Consanguinity

During and right after the Neolithic Age, civilized men of 8000 B.C. were largely under the control of the priesthood, advanced members of which had developed a high degree of deductive reasoning. Elaborate ceremonies and organized warfare were common in this era, and our management concepts and organizational structures have roots in this very ancient religious and military heritage. Conflict and fraternal association cause strong bonds of affinity between persons who experience the same situation. It is not necessary that they have a degree of family relationship, although this was often involved in the earlier organizations.

The United States, like most nations, is "clubby" by nature; the population forms and reforms itself into organizational groups to satisfy the human tendency to seek kindred souls with which to consort. Resonance is sought in all walks of life.

A recent study in Newburyport, Massachusetts, showed that 800 formal clubs and organizations existed among the 17,000 people in this area. Sociologists and psychologists find this tendency of birds of a feather to flock together a well-demonstrated factor in group dynamics, and the phenomenon is of value in the study of organizational behavior.

In the Second World War, John C. Flanagan, psy-

chologist for the testing service of the American Council
of Education, was put in charge of the Aviation Psychology
Program of the Army Air Force in an effort to match the
development of trained pilots with the development of
aircraft. Flanagan's staff found that in the high-risk bomb-
ing missions over Germany, where a flier had a 25 percent
chance of returning, one of the most important factors in
success was the sense of being a member of a group in
which flying and fighting were the only accepted ways of
behaving. Living, fighting, and playing together, with minimum contact with outside groups, identified these men
as a unit, and this bolstered their morale to the point
where it was a significant factor in their survival.

Perhaps modern business can take a leaf out of this
wartime "Flanagan's institute" and accentuate the need
for each manager's individual identification with an elite
team who are fighting for their free enterprise existence
against formidable odds of competition, government, in-
imical ideology, the capricious cycles of business, and international political and economic tensions. This feeling
of belonging and being in the inner circle by reason of
performance, competence, shared experiences, and shared
risks is a strong bond for a management team.

Resonance Within a System of Authority

Whatever the formal organization structure, the affinity of a certain inner group for each other can make or
break a management record of achievement.

In the middle of the spectrum of management systems
is the "system of authority" approach used by large inter-

national corporations, including Standard Oil Company of Ohio, Du Pont, Union Carbide, Monsanto, General Electric, General Motors, Imperial Chemical Industries, Unilever, Shell, Tata Ltd., and many others. The literature is replete with discussions of this combination of decentralized administration with centralized control.

This system seems to best fit gargantuan, complex organizations. However, its structural lubricity in the last analysis depends on the resonance of the decentralized groups (*a*) within themselves, (*b*) with the top management group in which control is centralized, and (*c*) with the supreme command that establishes broad policy. The "contrapuntal" elements, the "obbligato" section, the "arpeggio" efforts, the management "intervals," and the inversions of such intervals that exist in the full organizational orchestration must be in the same or a related key. They may be in different octaves on the scalar chain of the organization, but all must be in resonance. Like Beethoven's *Ninth Symphony*, the movements may be diverse, but in the end they must ring out a unified theme if the organization is to be effective. The all-important chief executive or conductor of this business symphony can accomplish this, if the respective members are resonant rather than dissonant in their relations with each other.

As industrialization and business complexities advance, the basis for a resonant managerial group moves further away from its ancestral roots of family or political background. Instead, resonance is begotten by a common ancestry with educational, intellectual, ethical, and professional strains which express themselves in the rapport that individual executive personalities establish when faced with a common objective in free enterprise business.

The Behaviorist's View

"It is probably most important for the leader to be socially sensitive to relevant dynamics of the follower whom he seeks to influence, including the follower's needs, feeling, and motivation, although sensitivity alone is not necessarily a guarantee of leadership effectiveness. His sensitivity to other entities is also important." In a collection of writings on the dynamics of leadership by Tannenbaum, Weschler, and Massarik, this quotation (5) concerns the principal *dramatis personae* of the leadership process: the leaders who wish to wield interpersonal influence and the followers whose attitudes and behavior are to be influenced.

The leader is concerned with his perceptual capacities or potential for response to stimuli from associates, followers, physical phenomena, and other external factors. His perceptual accuracy with respect to social factors—that is, his social sensitivity—depends on empathy, insight, and understanding, plus his diagnostic talents as related to followers and associates. As a manager completes his "cognitive perceptual structuring" of his associates, his followers, and the situation itself, there evolves what various researchers refer to as a "psychological map." This is either an explicit or an implicit visualization of the circumstances and the action pathways available.

A sound, empathetic, and resonant relationship is a rich asset for a manager. It is a dynamic matter requiring compassion and spiritual insight on the part of the manager in dealing with his associates and followers.

Someone once said that you can see farther through a tear than through a telescope. So it is with the perceptual capabilities of a top manager who leads a resonant group through understanding and voluntary allegiance: He must possess social sensitivity to the relevant dynamics of his associates and his followers.

In recent years, training of managers in the area of social sensitivity and behavioral flexibility has added a new dimension to human relations study. This sensitivity training is designed to help individuals to achieve a better understanding of themselves and others in the cultural situations they face in today's complex society.

Resonant Management Reproduction

This problem of having ready resonant back-up management in depth is the most fundamental problem in management today, because the rapid growth of free enterprise has outstripped the development of professional managers by the traditional evolutionary methods. A number of recent studies have dealt with the increasing shortage of executive talent available for positions in middle management—a shortage that will get considerably worse before it gets better.

Between 1955 and 1965, the number of corporate management positions in U.S. industry rose by 28 percent. There were 12 million males in the 35–44 age group in 1965, but despite total population increases there will be only 11.1 million in this same group in 1975. This last figure is directly attributable to the low birth rate during the decade from 1930 to 1940. When it is considered that the greater percentage of potential middle managers were born to educated middle-class families, the 11.1 million figure diminishes even more in its significance as a future pool for executive talent. Some thoughtful courses of action seem to be indicated for large U.S. corporations that wish to avoid the consequences of ignoring these facts.

In *Henry V* the Duke of Burgundy says, "The vine, the merry cheerer of the heart, unpruned, dies." Lack of care and cultivation of the vine causes the fruit to diminish in the same way that neglect of the roots of management in government, business, and industry causes a withering of key personnel and a thwarting of the management reproduction function. Men, because they so often believe themselves to be near-immortal, have trouble planning for the future leadership of a company. Yet, theoretically, a corporation is truly immortal as a legal entity and must provide for the consistent cultivation and blending of resonant groups of leaders.

Care and cultivation of the vine do not alone make for a great wine such as sherry, produced year after year with the same high quality and delightful flavor. The success of this famous Spanish wine lies in the Jerez *solera* system of blending.

The solera system was not defined by the Spanish authorities until 1932, although the wine had been made for many centuries. Perhaps with only 50 to 60 years of formally recognized scientific management activities in our country, a "solera" system for a resonant blending process in business management can be formulated to insure a consistent vintage manager crop that will possess adequate group affinity within its ranks.

Like the senior key men in an organization, the older sherries in the Jerez system provide the golden essence that must be blended with the new stock.

The bright future wines are observed, recognized, and classified for aging; the poorer new wines are relegated to routine outlets or dumped. So, too, does an experienced manager start his promising young men in general assignments, watching them (to assess their capabilities, their attributes, their interpersonal relations) and training them by means of special duties. Early culling and careful development are the secrets in both the Jerez solera system and our related management development system.

While fundamentally simple, this latter system involves one of the neglected techniques in management today. A consistently well-managed company reflects a foundation of early selection, cultivation, and elimination of individuals, plus a well-ordered hybridization of experienced talents that can work together to achieve top-quality results. The neglect in some companies lies not so much in the selection of promising young men as in the failure to guide them, to group them properly, to feature their strong points and talents, and to help them develop needed qualities.

In the solera method of wine production, only stocks that have been properly developed and tested for affinity to others find their way into the system. An individual solera consists of a number of casks that have an affinity for each other, all containing wine of the same type, style, age, and quality; a solera system consists of a number of individual soleras of the same style and type of wine but of different ages. If we could produce top-flight management crops year after year, in the manner of the viticulturist, we would offer to shareholders in our modern ventures a lineage, a resonant management team, and an accomplishment record second to none.

The cannibalistic era, when corporations could afford to swallow their human resources without replenishing their leadership reserves, ended years ago. Today's urgent need for executive talent is evidence that business and the educational institutions have failed to make the required changeover with anything approaching the flexibility and efficiency normally applied to problems with inanimate factors, or with the skills and organization necessary for the production of a regular vintage crop of qualified leaders.

This failure has led to severe losses in executive leadership and experience. In some instances, it has led to frustration of natural abilities within the personnel "stock," lessened incentive, and caused a decline in the supply of business pioneers. It also accounts for the rise in the number of executive transfers, as companies bid against each other for top talent, and it is perhaps one underlying factor in the current urge-to-merge vogue wherein management talents are acquired through the adoption technique.

If the cannibalistic trend is allowed to continue, the eventual result must be a rapid degeneration of our organized ability to produce and distribute consistently. Industry's apparent abandonment of the basic requirement to produce new leaders could foster a dependence on artificial economic props and stopgap management techniques that would sap the strength of business and its ability to survive even minor business setbacks and organizational reverses.

Resonant management reproduction should be more than a philosophy or a "solera system." It must be converted into a dynamic, vital force capable of repairing the depleted state of our leadership resources. The responsibility for the conversion and the structuring of the team falls on those charged with executive assignments.

As a concept, the synthesis of management talent—the

continuous critical selection, development, and resonant blending of organizational cadres so that they will reproduce as well as produce leaders—may have superficial overtones of viticulture. As a practice, however, it may well be the cure for the creeping atrophy of executive muscle that has become an international malady.

Improving Management Resonance

Starting with the proposition that resonance in the field of electricity and resonance in the field of management possess analogous values, we have reviewed the requirements for resonance, the character of resonance as it relates to the compatibility of individuals and to nepotism, some behavioral aspects of resonance, and the problem of management reproduction.

To believe that there is nothing new in this concept, or that the existence of resonance in management is a tired and obvious matter, is to ignore the opportunity for exploring the use of the resonance factor in a conscious way in organization management. The behavioral scientists have a chance here, provided research is continued on the phenomenon, to guide the manager in the use of new techniques.

The Catgut Acoustical Society is an informal organization, started in 1963, that publishes a semiannual newsletter and holds meetings. Prompted by the late Professor Frederick A. Saunders of the Harvard physics department and a colleague, Mrs. Carleen Maley Hutchins, the organization's objective is to improve the resonance of the violin, an instrument that supposedly reached a peak of perfection in the Renaissance. It is only recently that suitable acoustical equipment and testing devices have been available to permit research in this area.

The study began in 1937 and was first reported in the *Journal of the Acoustical Society of America,* but the problem of incorporating the experts' knowledge of the effects of violin wood and cavity resonance on tone quality was not worked out until 1960. Now, under the guidance of Mrs. Hutchins, a new family of eight fiddles, ranging from a treble violin 16 inches long to a contrabass 7 feet long, have been created in accordance with the defined principles of proper resonance for desired tone quality. In each of the eight frequency ranges there is an instrument that has the dynamics, the expressive qualities, and the overall power characteristic of the violin itself as compared to the viola, cello, and double bass.

If we can determine the anatomy of resonance in a management situation, and identify and arrange the key factors at will, just as has been done in violin research or electrical engineering, would this not provide valuable know-how for the managers? Some work is already under way in this field. Under the auspices of the Office of Naval Research, some interesting studies of leadership effectiveness in small groups have recently developed new knowledge, including a set of principles that may permit restructuring the job and its surrounding conditions to improve the resonance factor of the management group. (6)

Fred E. Fiedler, professor of psychology at the University of Illinois, has attacked the problem of making better use of the available management talent by engineering the job situation so as to adapt it to the style of the leader or leaders involved. His real-life studies dealt with military combat crews, basketball teams, surveying parties, steel workers, members of management, and boards of directors.

Programs studied in the United States and Belgium led to the conclusion that a great potential for improvement in the resonance factor exists through organizational planning and engineering: (*a*) The leader's position power can be enhanced by giving him subordinates and associates with varying degress of sole or joint authority to best suit his style of command. (*b*) The task at hand can be delineated or generalized, whichever is best to challenge the particular leader's style. And (*c*) the composition of the management group can be changed to alter the leader's relations with his men.

Application of these three principles to business management opens up new degrees of freedom for top management in maximizing the plus values of a high resonance quotient.

References

[1] R. Thouin, "The Selection of Higher-Grades Staff," *Management International Review* (1966/3), p. 13.

[2] W. I. Thomas, *The Unadjusted Girl* (Boston: Little, Brown & Co., 1923).

[3] Vance Packard, *The Pyramid Climbers* (New York: McGraw-Hill Book Co., 1962).

[4] David W. Ewing, "Is Nepotism So Bad?" *Harvard Business Review* (Jan.–Feb. 1965).

[5] Robert Tannenbaum, Irving R. Weschler, and Fred Massarik, *Leadership and Organization: A Behavioral Science Approach* (New York: McGraw-Hill Book Co., 1961), p. 37.

[6] Fred E. Fiedler, "Engineer the Job to Fit the Manager," *Harvard Business Review* (Sept.–Oct. 1965).

Pursue, keep up with, circle round and round your life, as a dog does his master's chaise. Do what you love. Know your own bone; gnaw at it, bury it, unearth it and gnaw it still.

—Henry David Thoreau

xii. A Way of Life

THE pursuit of the corporate way of life has led some student sons to label their executive fathers "workaholics," replacing Whyte's ideological appellation "organization man" of over a decade ago. Some business analysts loftily refer to the managerial breed as a "birth and mobile class" or the "podium climbers." Yale Professor Chris Argyris takes the lid off the corporate structure and sees organizational behavior as part of a "living system." Harvard Professor David C. McClelland designates the phenomenon as part of his "achieving society," while the classical anthropologists stick to their "culture" nomenclature to describe the executive life in terms of motivations, status, values, rights, and *modus vivendi*. Stephen Potter contributes "bitzleish" or "oneupman" as a name for the successful operator who gets away with it "in the smaller world of Life . . . without being an absolute Plonk." Vance Packard writes of the executive class as existing in a "veiled and curious world," and so it is for those on the outside of the organizational pyramid.

For those on the inside, the current way of life is a behavior pattern that is appropriate to this particular period on the time scale of management evolution. The common denominator is transition, for the mores of the manager change along with society. And it is axiomatic that changes will occur that steadily impinge on the manager's style of living. The manager changes and the environment changes; the successful life style of the former manager may or may not fit the needs of the manager of today's or tomorrow's enterprise. Thus a constant attitude of inquiry toward these behavioral patterns is an essential element in the managerial way of life.

Moral Authority

"The manner of operation of the social insects—the ants, the bees, and the termites—has been the envy of dictators and would-be dictators," wrote Floyd A. Harper. "In the pattern of these insects is found their ideal of an 'orderly and industrious' society of humans. Every aspiring dictator, both large and small, would like to ascend to the throne of 'queen bee' of a worldwide human colony, in which every human would become subservient to the dictator's own wishes and would serve his plan with unwavering loyalty." (1) The bee culture and the managerial culture do have certain orderly and industrious aspects in common, and the manager must have some of the dictator's talents in his makeup. The power wielded by a dictator or a professional manager is tremendous and frightening to some people, and it is the source of much of the lore that surrounds the manager.

The power of the manager is real and is based in part on what may be called "moral authority." Moral authority

as a power is not unlike the power possessed by intellectu-
als who can speak with general authority about a subject
in which they have no particular competence. A journalist
speaking about the press, an engineer discoursing on super-
highways, or a business leader talking on business are pro-
fessionals at work in their own spheres. But the manager,
like the intellectual, because of his position in the hierarchy of a powerful economic unit somehow carries his
authority over in other fields despite his lack of specific
competence in them. This moral authority is a powerful
force and is a part of the current culture of the managerial
class.

Managerial Myths

Myths about management persist today, not only outside the managerial community but also among its practitioners. Products of fads and fashions, of half-truths and
attractive oversimplifications, these myths influence both
executives and the public in varying degrees. Sixteen such
managerial myths, ranging from the subject of the over-
worked executive to the expense account and the impact
on the individual, were scrutinized carefully in *The Folklore of Management,* a book by the late Clarence B.
Randall, former president of Inland Steel. (2)
"Everyone writes about business except the businessman," Randall said, and then he proceeded to puncture
the fables and folklore that have built up through the
years. It takes only a few indiscreet or immature businessmen to create an adverse image for this entire sector of
society and add credibility to a particular myth of man-

agerial behavior that may have press and public appeal.

Mason Locke Weems was the early nineteenth-century Episcopalian parson mainly responsible for the anecdotal Sunday School image of George Washington as a cherry tree chopper. Weems has some twentieth-century counterparts who take a snapshot view of the executive suite or the managerial class and develop it into an image that really does not fit the facts of executive life.

The complexities of business and the behavior of the manager are the constant target of journalists in search of "cherry tree" explanations that will attract readers. The need for communication between managers and the other key segments of society is critical, and must be met, if there are to be understanding and respect for the "veiled and curious world of the executive."

It is well known—and has been pointed out in this book—that the prestige of the executive or businessman among the general public is not as high as that of his contemporaries in government, science, and university life. When the University of Chicago's National Opinion Research Center (3) surveyed "occupational prestige in the United States," the first nine occupations on the list— as ranked—were Supreme Court justice, 1; physician, 2; nuclear physicist, 3.5; scientist, 3.5; government scientist, 5.5; state governor, 5.5; cabinet member in the federal government, 8; college professor, 8; and U.S. representative in Congress, 8. (See also Chapter VIII.)

The report points out that financial power does not result in high status. Three occupations that illustrated this were as follows: board member in a large corporation, 17.5; banker, 24.5; and owner of a factory that employs about 100 people, 31.5.

And You're Another!

Operation Dialogue is a lively program that has been sponsored by American Management Association in recent years as an attempt to clear up areas of misunderstanding among various sectors of society, particularly as they affect the business community. It has as its goal the furtherance of the free enterprise way of life.

It is interesting to note that those who take part in Operation Dialogue and who do not represent the business sector often characterize businessmen as lacking social responsibility. For example, the comments of some of the 1967 participants reflected this belief:

- There are "no big statues" to businessmen.
- Businessmen lack a basic notion of their mission.
- Business operates as a closed society.
- Business operates with the inhumanity of scientists, without respect for human values.
- Business manipulates men.
- The ethic of power predominates.

But managers are not the only ones who take their lumps in these sessions. Those participants who are not academicians say this sort of thing with respect to educators:

- They put forth too much propaganda in the classroom.
- They have the habit of passing judgment on business with no background.
- They pursue the ethic of knowledge.

- When you can't succeed in education, you become a guidance counselor.
- They pursue literacy rather than wisdom.
- Academic freedom is a closed union.

Dialoguers of all stripes go on to say, with respect to the youth of the nation, that

- They are more interested in poetry than in progress.
- Youth are right today for no reason.
- They are not concerned with the structure or the stability of society.
- They are concerned only with change.
- Their new "good" is personal satisfaction of the individual.
- They have no idea where money comes from.
- There is a general depravity in young society.

Participants who are not clergymen argue in these terms about theologians:

- They are bankrupt.
- There is too big a gap between the pulpit and the pew.
- They are trying to make morality profitable.

And the non-fourth-estate participants say of the press that

- The current practice of trial by press is unsatisfactory.
- There is a new ignorance revolution.

- The kooks are taking over, not the leaders of the press.

The Operation Dialogue program presents cogent evidence that managers are not alone in being categorized on the basis of the behavior of a few atypical members. But the myths of management still lurk in the lobby, and the manager must shoulder responsibility for correcting misconceptions of the corporate way of life as soon as he himself recognizes what actual discernible patterns of behavior do exist in his sphere of activity and, more importantly, as soon as he appreciates that they are constantly changing.

Education and Communication

Today's *modus vivendi* for a manager is one in which education plays an immense role. Education, in fact, has become the task of our times. With so much knowledge now available to the manager, knowledge that he formerly would have had to acquire the hard way, by experience, the manager's particular task—indeed, his whole way of life—becomes one of a challenging educational process for himself and his organization.

The explosive growth of organizations that provide management education is testimony to this impact of education on the manager and his way of life. The opportunity to learn about management matters before experiencing them is a turnabout from earlier days, and many old-timers who are still active in the executive ranks find it difficult to appreciate that the new way of life is different in terms of its educational conditioning and its future demands on the executive. He now faces a different set of survival problems, but he is equipped with a formidable armament in the form of management science techniques and a more enlightened understanding of the behavioral basics that underlie this way of life.

If all managers could utilize all the managerial know-how that is readily available to them now, there would be fewer ulcers, fewer business failures, and fewer career casualties. As we have said, the challenge of the manager today is to manage as well as he makes. He is no longer primarily concerned with making or selling goods and services; rather, he is concerned with becoming sufficiently educated in management science and its techniques and limitations to add this capability to his own artful exercise of instinct and his particular experiences in managing the enterprise.

A dynamic organization requires a leader; otherwise it will spin its wheels. The leader, in turn, must have a team. He must tell the members of this team where he is headed and convince them that the chosen destination is a good place for them to go and that he is the proper leader to take them there. In large organizations, therefore, the communication problem becomes dominant because the leader's goals and dreams must be communicated effectively to those about him and they must then infect the others with the same enthusiasm and determination.

Leadership Is the Key

The world will go on somehow, and more crises will follow. It will go on best, however, if among us there are men who have stood apart, who refused to be anxious or too much concerned, who were cool and inquiring and had their eyes on a longer past and a longer future. By their example, they can remind us that the passing moment is only a moment. By their loyalty, they will have cherished those things which only the disinterested mind can use.

—WALTER LIPPMANN

The disinterested mind is perhaps more appropriate to a historian than to a forward-looking manager whose commitment is more to the future than to the past. Nevertheless, a realistic perspective on the manager's leadership responsibility and opportunity is most important. Authority and knowledge have for years past been the basis for leadership. The orchestration of an organization is an art form that only recently has been aided by management science skills and techniques.

Leadership is difficult to define universally, for the organization, the circumstance, and the field of activity are all involved. Holbrook Jackson, an English journalist before the turn of the century, stated that "in democracies, those who lead follow; those who follow lead"—and Will Rogers added an ironic twist to this viewpoint when he said that "no party is as bad as its leaders."

The officeholder's official title theoretically tells the world that he is a leader, but there have been serious challenges to this presumption. In the case of community leadership, Floyd Hunter's studies have shown that position does not always identify the leader, for in some communities government is actually conducted by a covert economic elite. Because of the variations in terminology characteristic of different associations and organizations in designing similar offices, a title may have little value in identifying the true leader. (4)

The reputational approach to identifying leaders is also open to question, since it does not measure leadership per se. Moreover, sociologists do not feel that a reputation for power is a valid index or yardstick of power in running things.

The decisional approach is preferred by many who would identify the leader. It involves tracing actions in regard to decision making and policy making. Yet decision making by a power holder may or may not reflect true leadership; it may be merely power wielding. The identification of a true leader is, in brief, a complex job of analyzing his track record.

The Chief Executive Sets the Pattern

Within the "living system" of management, the head of the enterprise sets the style and the patterns of behavior of those within the organization.

A recent study of U.S. presidents reported in *News Front* (5) reveals some interesting traits in these men. Here the 250 "best-managed U.S. corporations" were characterized as those having the best sales increase, the best percentage of profit to sales, and the best percentage of profit to shareholder's equity. Not surprisingly, problems of human relations were the major concern of these corporations' presidents. There really was no "average" chief executive. However, the prototype that did emerge from this computer-programmed study, which was followed up by lengthy questionnaires on working habits and personal formulas of success, gives a snapshot of the top corporate executive and his way of life.

Some of the findings were as follows:

- There is no time clock for presidents.
- The average age was 53, although the spread went from 37 to 86 years of age.
- Only 18 percent of the men were Ivy Leaguers, and 14 percent didn't reach college.
- More than a quarter do ten hours of homework a week and spend two evenings on business away from home. The average work week was 55 hours.
- Most of these presidents are early risers and late leavers.
- They all gripe about too much paperwork, and most of them report that they have 5 to 10 group meetings and 20 to 25 individual meetings every week.
- They complain about being able to spend less than five hours in the marketplace and about the need to spend ten hours a week studying internal reports and three to five hours keeping up with outside publications.
- Interestingly, only 38 percent have an official executive assistant. Most of them have five to ten men reporting directly to them. They are all strongly in favor of delegating, particularly for fact finding.
- They deliver speeches on the average of one a month.
- Three-fourths serve as directors of other companies, and they devote four hours a week to school, hospital, charitable, and civic affairs.
- Their average annual salary was $100,000, though with a wide range, including bonus and stock options.
- Almost all own their own homes; only 10 percent are cliffdwellers in rented quarters.

- Three-fourths own valuable art and sculpture.
- Of course, almost all have two cars—Cadillacs, Lincolns, and Oldsmobiles in that order.
- Almost all these men feel that they have paid a heavy price for their success, and 64 percent admit that they achieved their position at considerable expense of time with their families.
- They have favorite hobbies of the usual varieties —golf, fishing, and boating—but, surprisingly, they are not generally avid readers.
- They characterize their essential chore as selecting, leading, and motivating the few top performers in their organizations (perhaps only 2 percent of the total).

The way of life portrayed in this composite cannot be called "typical," since the average executive loses the individuality that makes managers such interesting and influential creatures. Nevertheless, the range of characteristics shown here definitely sets the executive suite in a class by itself, exclusive in comparison with other sectors of society.

All in all, it seems that the manager's way of life is one in which the leader is obsessed with his role in the same way that Charles Darwin implied when he stated: "It is a cursed evil to any man to become so absorbed in any subject as I am in mine." Mark Twain put it another way: "Your true pilot cares nothing about anything on earth but the river, and his pride in his occupation surpasses the pride of kings."

For a manager to be successful, then, he must learn that the leader's way of life means adjusting to constant change and is an all-encompassing and demanding existence. As President Harry Truman so pungently remarked, "If he can't stand the heat, he should get out of the kitchen."

References

[1] Floyd A. Harper, *Liberty: A Path to Its Recovery* (Irvington-on-Hudson, N.Y.: Foundation for Economic Education, 1949), p. 62.

[2] Clarence B. Randall, *The Folklore of Management* (Boston: Little, Brown and Company, 1961).

[3] Philip H. Abelson, "Prestige," *Science* (Aug. 1964).

[4] Floyd Hunter, *Community Power Structure* (Chapel Hill: University of North Carolina Press, 1953), p. 82.

[5] "Private Lives of Company Presidents," *News Front* (May 1967).

Additional Readings

William V. D'Antonio and Howard J. Ehrlich, eds., *Power and Democracy in America* (South Bend, Ind.: Notre Dame University Press, 1961).

Chris Argyris, "Behavioral Scientist at Large," *The Conference Board Record* (May 1967).

Edward A. McCreary, *The Americanization of Europe* (New York: Doubleday & Company, Inc., 1964).

David Granick, *The European Executive* (New York: Doubleday & Company, Inc., 1962).

Barry M. Richman, "Soviet Management in Transition," *MSU Business Topics* (Spring 1967).

Summary

XIII. Axioms of Management

*T*HE principles we have been discussing might be called axioms of management. They are principles that apply not only to the current state of management but to new experiences that will be encountered by the manager in the future.

Management science can provide a professional approach to the basic principles that support the body of specialized knowledge we call management. But to try to focus management lore into scientific terms at this stage of the art's development is perhaps premature and certainly ambitious. The individual manager must therefore consciously seek the truths that lie buried in the pattern of his own managerial behavior. The axioms thus identified may assist him in his career of service as a manager.

It is true, of course, that axioms change. Some are discarded and are replaced with more modern versions, and new axioms are added as management art and science are more closely examined. However, while recognizing that some mutations will occur as the economic and social constraints on the manager change, we can still isolate certain principles that are axiomatic and that present a challenge for the manager to consider, use, refine, and supplement as he gains personal experience.

Once the manager has developed an intellectual interest in the body of management knowledge that is rapidly being accumulated and refined, a second step becomes obvious: that of intellectual inquiry into the management discipline. This requires a conscious effort to identify what is constant and what are the worthy common denominators. These principles form the foundation of the responsible role that satisfies the ethical, social, and intellectual needs of the manager who deserves his title.

The history of mathematics seems to have started uncertainly in the period of the Ionian Greeks (600 B.C.). Thereafter, it took about 300 years until Euclid could state his 15 famous axioms to support the concepts of geometry. Other axioms were set up in the books of Genesis, Exodus, Leviticus, and Deuteronomy; these are constantly being tested in the turbulent life we lead today as individuals and managers. Three of these axioms from the Bible might be stated as follows in paraphrased form:

- God created the earth, the life, and the people, and they belong to Him. The manager's social profile and the proper use of executive authority will recognize this.
- The greatest difference in the world is the difference between right and wrong. Managerial and individual ethics and the power factor deal with this interface.
- The greatest value in this life is the single individual; the human being is priceless. A manager's knowledge of behavioral basics guides him in this value system.

With scientific management only about threescore years old, it would be presumptuous to expect to pull out of the omnium-gatherum of facts, cases, and techniques any axioms as profound as these Biblical truths or the work of Euclid. It was not until the turn of the century that mathematicians themselves dug very deeply into questions of principle. As Swift remarked of the mathematicians of Laputa in *Gulliver's Travels,* they were unpardonably hazy about first principles and resorted to faith or, in some cases, an uncanny sort of instinct. Faith and instinct will undoubtedly remain important to managers because they can sometimes penetrate the soft-science side of managing in the free enterprise system.

The problem of the executive is to get people about him to help him get maximum results with a minimum of friction. Charles Steinmetz put it in this way: "Cooperation is not a sentiment; it is an economic necessity."

To whatever extent the management axioms that follow are understood and obeyed, we have cooperation, harmony, and profitable service. Since the greatest waste of management time is not the loss of the time itself but its wrong use, these axioms may be as valuable for what is left out as for what is included.

The anatomy of risk. The job of the manager is to create values by taking risks in our social and economic order. The manager must be able to recognize and distinguish between risk situations and uncertain situations in order to maximize opportunity.

Managerial instinct. After all the alternatives in a decision-making situation have been examined in a professional manner, the ingredient of management instinct —which often lies dormant, even in most experienced executives—can often tip the balance in favor of success. A dangerous misuse of this attribute is to apply instinct impulsively to decisions when a high probability of certainty is present among several choices. The polishing of instinct for use in situations of true uncertainty is a challenge for the individual manager bent on self-improvement.

Management—art or science? A combination of scientific discipline with the freedom of art will make the manager's effort acceptable to those who must react to it and interact with it. Such a combination is truly the work of a professional, who can do for his livelihood what others do for pleasure. The combination of scientific thinking with art in management also can preserve the balance of order while allowing enough disorder to encourage innovation and prevent decay.

The managementality gap. Although realistic politicians have analyzed situations before making vital decisions since Machiavelli's time, business managers constantly make decisions with inadequate information and under the pressures of insufficient time. Too few managers have reached the point where they rigorously analyze alternative consequences before choosing one solution over another. A prime problem is the different mental attitudes of those involved—today's top executives as opposed to the more recent management-oriented technical graduates. The potential contributions of management science to the business process are limited by the gap between the mentality of management-science practitioners and that of currently successful managers. Both face the challenge of developing interaction, mutual trust, and commitment. The disparate talents of the charismatic intuitive leader, the management scientist, and the behavioral scientist must be welded to help close the managementality gap.

Survival of the fittest. The selection processes of the management maze require the manager to be able to cope with the principle of equal opportunity and the principle of unequal rank and status. A healthy system results, but the executive fallout that accompanies it is unfortunate. Knowledge of the anatomy of this phenomenon will help guide a heads-up manager to a level of achievement consistent with his capabilities.

Executive authority. Organized society forms the basis for executive authority, which is an extension of the right of private property. A professional manager is required to act as a trustee for the whole of society to preserve this position over the long term in our free enterprise system. He must be conscious of the legitimate role he is playing when he acts as a trustee for others. The theory of management's reserved rights establishes the supremacy of management authority in all matters except those expressly conceded. When management attains a real professional status in the eyes of the public, it will be self-evident that his acceptance of a trust from society legitimatizes his executive functions.

The catalyst: profit. Private enterprise dies unless the manager can continually justify its existence by performing a service and making a profit at the same time. Profit as the potential reward catalyzes the acceptance of risk to gain that reward and is necessary to an advancing democratic social order. Profit is the ignition key to the economic engine that is so vital to our system. Managers must recognize that profit is respectable and use its catalytic value properly.

The social profile. The social and economic order operating under free enterprise requires an overt personal response from the manager if the larger social system is to be preserved. The apparent dichotomy of the manager's responsibility to his enterprise and to society as a whole may represent dual short-term objectives, but these coalesce on a longer time scale into the single purpose of maintaining and developing our order in the free enterprise way of life. The manager must accept this social profile.

Behavioral basics. One of the most controversial aspects of management has to do with the use of behavioral science to minister to people's needs and organizational relationships. Some knowledge of this discipline helps the manager to deal with the human actions and reactions that result whenever two or more people come together. This is a misty area of know-how for the executive; nevertheless, proper control of the soft-science elements of the enterprise will insure the profitable existence of its hard-science side. The manager should understand these distinctions.

The powers that be. A true test of the professional manager's greatness is his intelligent use of the power that accrues to him by virtue of his position. Inspirational power, properly directed, also is necessary to his continuing success. With power in hand, in mind, and in heart, a manager can function in a balanced manner, serving his enterprise, the welfare of society, and his own career objectives.

The resonance factor. The ability of a manager to adjust personally to his colleagues' styles and moods harmoniously will stabilize the organization and assist him in achieving both the goals of the enterprise and his own career goals. Recognition of this resonance requirement is a necessity for the manager.

A way of life. The behavior patterns of the managerial class are focused around change and transition as their mores mutate with those of society in general. Constant inquiry into these behavioral patterns and their value systems is necessary if a manager is to keep his personal equilibrium. When he is swept into the executive way of life, the emotional investment is great, and this investment must be professionally controlled.

Index

Abegglen, James, 90, 93
achieving society, concept of, 199
American Brake Shoe Co., 46-47
American business, ethics of, 129-132
American Council of Education, 187
American Management Association, 105, 134, 203
Ansoff, Igor, 70
anti-management scientist reaction, 77
Appley, Lawrence A., 105-106, 134
Ardrey, Robert, 36
Argyris, Chris, 153, 199
attitude change, need for, 80
authority: executive, 219; moral, 200-201; resonance within, 188-189
authority system, 188
Avery, Sewell, 41
Aviation Psychology Program, 188
axioms, defined, 216-217

Balchin, Nigel, 25
Barnard, Chester I., 42, 49
Bavelas, Alex, 47
behavior: studies of, 143-144, 154-159; technical change and, 145-147
behavioral basics, 139-159; business application of, 153-154; value system and, 216, 220
behavioral science: defined, 142-143; in management, 147-153; research in, 153; resonance and, 190-191
Benedict, St., 179
Berelson, Bernard, 142
Bethlehem Steel Corp., 41
Bierce, Ambrose, 27
Big Business, power in, 168
Blake, Robert, 85
Boulding, Kenneth, 91
Boyle, Robert, 55
Brandeis University, 69
Braybrooke, David, 41-42

Bright, James R., 19-20
Brody, Rodney H., 20
Buddha, 172
Burnham, James, 162-163
business: ethics of, 129-132; gambling as, 27-28; motivating factors in, 128-129; national purpose and, 124-127; reasons for entering, 128-129; survival in, 96-98
Business Ethics Advisory Council, 130
business leaders, study of, 89-90, 93-94
Business Week, 141, 149

Cambridge University, 55
Cannon, Walter B., 91
career mobility, 93-94
Carnegie, Andrew, 126, 147
Carnegie, Dale, 145
Carnegie Institute of Technology, 155
Carnegie-Mellon University, 70
Catgut Acoustical Society, 195
Chamberlin, Neil W., 91
change, rapidity of, 66-67
Chase, Stuart, 143, 175
Chicago, University of, 202
Cicero, 23-24
civilization, business and, 125
Clark, Wallace, 151
clubs and organizations, 187
Code of Hammurabi, 125
Colgate Psychological Laboratory, 45
collective bargaining, 108
Commerce Department, 40
communication: education and, 205-206; problems of, 74; scientist and, 82
computer error, 20
computer hardware, obsolescence of, 76
computer mystique, 75
computer power, 67

Connor, John T., 40
Copeman, George, 155
corporation: authority system in, 188-189; commitment to, 82; family management in, 186; programmed study of, 208-211
cronyism, 183

Darwin, Charles, 34, 96, 210
decision: bad, 65; calculus of, 63
decision making, 28-31
decision theory, 78
Delphi technique, 37, 68
democracy: business and, 129; free enterprise and, 104, 186
Dennison, Henry S., 152
Department of Defense, 17
Dickson, W. J., 149
Dommermuth, William P., 94
Drucker, Peter F., 31, 104

education: business and, 125-126; communication and, 205-206; opportunity and, 93
Emerson, Harrington, 150
Engels, Friedrich, 114
error: defined, 19; forecasting and, 26; margin of, 18-19
ethics, of American business, 129-132
evolution, theory of, 96-97
executive: pattern set by, 208-211; two cultures of, 80-81; *see also* manager
executive authority, 103-112
executive behavior, 133-134
executive leadership, loss of, 194

family management, resonance and, 186-187
fears, as impediment to success, 95-96
Federal Reserve Board, 26
feedback system, management and, 79-80
Fiedler, Fred E., 196
Firestone, Harvey, 147
Flanagan, John C., 187
Follett, Mary Parker, 56
Ford, Henry, 147-148
Ford Foundation, 142
Fortune, 167

Foy, Fred C., 117
Frankel, Victor, 133
free enterprise system, democracy and, 104, 186
Freud, Sigmund, 28
future, forecasting of, 26-27

Galileo Galilei, 172
Galvin, Robert W., 117
Gantt charts, 151-152
Gantt, Henry Laurence, 55-56, 151-152
Gardner, John, 166
Gaulle, Gen. Charles de, 66
Gavin, Gen. James M., 119
General Motors Corp., 157-158, 163
General Motors Export Corp., 150
Gestalt psychology, 50
Gilbreth, Lillian M., 56
Given, William B., Jr., 46-47
Glacier Metals Co., 154
Grotjohn, Martin, 45
group dynamics, 187-188

habit, vs. instinct, 31
Haire, Mason, 91
Harper, Floyd A., 200
Harvard Business Review, 185
Harvard Business School, 40, 154
Harvard Medical School, 91
Harvard University, 119
Hawkins, Anthony Hope, 75
Hawthorne experiment, 149
Hayes, Isaac Israel, 34
Helmer, Olaf, 37
Herzberg, Frederick, 153
Higginson, George, 91
Hitler, Adolf, 97
Hooke, Robert, 55
Hopf, Harry, 151
Hower, Ralph M., 91
Hoxie, R. F., 56
Hughes Tool Company, 20
human error, 20; *see also* error
Hunter, Floyd, 207
Hutchins, Carleen Maley, 195

Illinois, University of, 196
Indiana, University of, 126
Industrial Revolution, 126

instinct, 40; emotion and, 35-36; human behavior and, 37-40; interpersonal relationships and, 44-48; intuition and, 39-41; limitations of, 41-44; as management axiom, 48-51; managerial, 217-218; motivation and, 37; origin of, 33-35; primary, 35-39; programming and, 37
Institute for Social Research, 144, 153
intuition: in management science, 77; vocation and, 42-43
intuitive reasoning, limitations of, 68-69

Jackson, Holbrook, 39, 207
James, William, 18
Jerez blending system, 192-194
Jesus Christ, 172
Johnson, Lyndon B., 64
Johnson, Brig. Gen. Robert Wood, 43
Johnson, Samuel, 171
Johnson & Johnson, 43
Juran, J. M., 146

Kennedy, John F., 143
Kettering, Charles F., 157
Knauth, Oswald, 91
Koontz, Harold, 140
Koppers Company, 117

labor-management rights, 108-110
Laird, Donald A., 45
leadership: defined, 207; personal vs. organizational, 47; resonance and, 194; stud factor in, 181-183
Le Châtelier, Henry, 158
Lehman, Harvey C., 92
Lerner, Max, 69
Likert, Rensis, 144, 153
Lincoln, Abraham, 64
Lippmann, Walter, 207
Little, Arthur D., Inc., 66, 119
Lorenz, Konrad, 37

McClelland, D. C., 199
McDonald, John, 27, 167
McFarland, Dalton E., 92
McFarlane, Alexander H., 16
McGregor, Douglas, 153, 171

McGuire, Joseph, 91
Machiavelli, Niccoló, 61, 166
man, behavioral characteristics of, 139-140
management: agreement and obligations in, 107-108; art vs. science in, 53-58; axioms of, 215-221; behavioral basics of, 139-159; behavioral science and, 147-153; choice in, 57-58; computer and, 57; consumer preference and, 26; criticism of, 123-124; defined, 105-108; feedback system and, 79-80; political aspects of, 78; power delegation in, 168-169; professional, 105, 111; profit and, 118-120; public opinion and, 111; resonance in, 180-183; social profile of, 123-134; social sciences and, 54; stockholders and, 108; success in, 61-62; systems approach to, 65-66; theory vs. practice in, 62
managementality gap, 61-85, 218; closing of, 79-85
management by crony, 183-184
management control, 69-70
management positions, number of, 191-192
management science, 62; application of, 215-216; communications problems in, 74; engineering and, 74; experience in, 77; industry and, 81; need for, 69-72; reaction against, 77; top management view of, 72-79
management scientists, common mission of, 84
management skill, technical obsolescence and, 72
management style, 81
management theory, behavior and, 140-141
manager: errors of, 22; half life of, 73; leadership of, 47, 181-183, 194, 207; life span of, 98-99; opportunity vs. rank or status of, 99-101; policy making by, 78-79; power of, 162-163, 168-170; resonance in, 176; riskmanship of, 31; Social Register and, 184-185; as trustee, 115-116
managerial instinct, 33-51

managerial myths, 201-202
managerial revolution, 163
manufacturing, techniques of, 25
Maremont, Arnold H., 126
margin of error, 22-23; *see also* error
Marks, Simon, 18-19
Martin, Edmund F., 41
Marx, Karl, 114
Maslow, A. H., 34-35, 46
Massarik, Fred, 190
mathematics, axioms in, 216-217
Maytag Co., 156
Mead, Shepherd, 36
Mere, Chevalier de, 28
Michigan, University of, 144
Miller, J. Irwin, 126
Mills, F. C., 25
Mitchell, Wesley C., 27
Monsanto Company, 65, 71
Montagu, M. F. Ashley, 139
Montgomery Ward & Co., 41, 65
Mooney, James David, 150
moral authority, 200-201
moral trusteeship principle, 126
Morris Motors, Ltd., 38
Mortimer, Charles G., 120-121
motivation: factors in, 128-129; instinct and, 34-37
Motorola, Inc., 117
Muller, Herbert J., 126
Mumford, Ethel Watts, 171
myths, managerial, 201-202

Napoleon I, 177
National Bureau of Economic Research, 27
National Industrial Conference Board, 126
natural selection, in business, 96-99
nepotism, 184-187
Neumann, John von, 68
Newman, Louis E., 142
Newton, Sir Isaac, 53, 55
Nicholson, Harold, 160
Nuffield, William Richard, 1st Viscount, 38

Office of Naval Research, 155, 196
Ogilvy, David, 44

one-upmanship, 82-83, 199
Operation Dialogue, 203-205
Opinion Research Corporation, 132
opportunity, education and, 93
organization: behavior in, 145-147; biological models of growth in, 91; power in, 167-170
Orth, Charles D., 91
Oxford University, 55

Packard, Vance, 199
Parkinson, C. Northcote, 89
Pascal, Blaise, 27
patents, number of, 67
Person, Harlow Stafford, 152
PERT (Program Evaluation and Review Technique), 70
Phillips Petroleum Co., 64
Plato, 56
policy making, manager in, 78
Potter, Stephen, 199
Potter, Van Rensselaer, 56
power: defined, 161-162; ethics and, 171-172; moral authority and, 200-201; nature and forms of, 161-172; in organization, 167-168; theories of, 165; of vested interests, 166; wielders of, 168-171
power groups, 165-166
praxiology, 141
production, profit and, 120-121
profit: as catalyst, 113-122, 219; excess, 117; as motivation, 114, 118-120, 128; production and, 120-121; as regulating function, 114; use of, 117
profit motive, in capitalism, 114-115, 128
project simulation, 71
psychological map, 190
Pythagoras, 172

Queeny, Edgar Monsanto, 111

Randall, Clarence B., 201
RAND Corp., 37-38, 66
Reisman, David, 165
Renaissance Executive, 100
resonance, 175-197; behavior and, 190-

191, 220; blending and, 192; defined, 176; improving of, 195-197; requirements for, 177-180; stud factor and, 180-183
resonant management reproduction, 191-195
retailing techniques, 25
Richelieu, Louis François Armand, Duc de, 178
Riley, John W., 127
risk: anatomy of, 15-31; defined, 16
Roethlisberger, Fritz, 149
Rogers, Will, 207
Roosevelt, Theodore, 15
Royal Society, London, 55
Russell, Bertrand, 161-162, 172

Sampson, Robert C., 148, 153, 164, 172
Saunders, Frederick A., 195
Savage, Charles H., Jr., 145
Scheff, Thomas J., 169
Schell, Erwin, 44
Schwab, Charles M., 41
science, social vs. natural, 55-57
scientist: self-management by, 83-84; two cultures of, 80-81
Scoutten, E. F., 156
Selekman, Benjamin M., 163
self-management, in scientists, 83-84
Shaw, George Bernard, 182
sherry wine, blending of, 192-194
Six Mistakes of Man, 23-24
Slichter, Sumner, 116
Sloan, Alfred P., Jr., 157-158
Smithcraft Corp., 142
Social Register, 184-185
social science: behavior and, 142; management and, 54-56; see also behavioral science
"solera" system of blending, 192-194
Southern California, University of, 140
Standard Oil Co. of California, 64
Stanger, Ross, 168
Steiner, Gary, 142
Steinmetz, Charles P., 217
stockholders, management responsibility to, 108
stud factor, resonance and, 180-183

success, impediments to, 95-96
Sullivan, J. W. N., 90
survival, advancement and, 92
survival of fittest, 219
Swift, Jonathan, 217

Tacitus, 24
Tannenbaum, Robert, 190
Taylor, Frederick W., 105, 148
technological change, 19-21
tenure, survival and, 94-95
Theory X and Theory Y concept, 153, 171
Thoreau, Henry David, 199
trade associations, 125
Truman, Harry S., 211
trust concept, property rights and, 110
Twain, Mark, 210

unions, rights of, 108-109
United States Office of Naval Research, 155, 196
Urwick, Lyndall F., 140, 158

Vanderbilt, Cornelius, 147
Vinci, Leonardo da, 77
violins, acoustical research in, 195-196
völkisch concept, Hitler's, 97
Vroom, Victor H., 153

Wald, Abraham, 75
Ward, Seth, 55
Warner, W. Lloyd, 90, 93
Washington, George, 202
WASPs (white Anglo-Saxon Protestants), 184
Weems, Mason Locke, 201
Weschler, Irving R., 190
Western Electric Co., 149
Western Management Science Institute, 155
Whitman, C. O., 37
Wiener, Norbert, 148
Wilde, Oscar, 33
women, power of, 171
Wren, Christopher, 55
Wright Air Development Center, 21

About the Author

ROBERT KIRK MUELLER, a senior professional at Arthur D. Little, Inc., is a director of its Zurich, Brussels, and London affiliates, a director and executive committee member of the Massachusetts Mutual Life Insurance Company, and a director of Baystate Corporation.

Formerly a director, executive committee member, and vice-president of the Monsanto Company, Mr. Mueller served as director of Monsanto's Brussels, London, and Toronto affiliates. He was president and board chairman of the Shawinigan Resins Corporation, general manager of Monsanto's plastics division, plant manager of the Longhorn Ordnance Works, and a vice-president and director of the American Management Association, of which he is a Life Member and a member of its World Council.

Mr. Mueller received his B.S. degree in chemical engineering from Washington University and a master's degree from the University of Michigan. He is a frequent lecturer and the author of *Effective Management Through Probability Controls* (Funk & Wagnalls). He is a Fellow of the Institute of Directors (London), a Fellow of the American Association for the Advancement of Science, and a member of the New York Academy of Sciences, American Chemical Society, American Institute of Chemical Engineers, and Society of the Chemical Industry. He serves as director of the Council of International Progress in Management (an affiliate of CIOS), a trustee of Colby Junior College (New London, New Hampshire), and a member of the Business Advisory Council of the School of Business Administration at the University of Massachusetts.